THE POWER OF SECRETS

RON E. STEPHENS

authorHOUSE®

AuthorHouse™
1663 Liberty Drive
Bloomington, IN 47403
www.authorhouse.com
Phone: 1-800-839-8640

First published by AuthorHouse 12/3/2010

ISBN: 978-1-4520-4354-8 (sc)

Library of Congress Control Number: 2010909599

Printed in the United States of America
Bloomington, Indiana

This book is printed on acid-free paper.

All scriptures are from the King James Version of the Bible unless otherwise indicated.
Other translations used:NLT – New Living Translation
NKJV – New King James Version
NIV – New International Version
AV – Amplified Version

DEDICATION

To my best friend, Dorretta, who has given me three beautiful children—Sophia, Sarah, and Sam—who helped me to understand the power of secrets.

ACKNOWLEDGMENTS

To Ron Fultz who understood my vision for this book from the very beginning. I told him I was writing a book on secrets, and every Sunday he bugged and encouraged me to complete the book. Thanks Ron, I appreciate you.

To Portia Simpson who was the mastermind-organizer. She helped me find a publisher, stay on track, arranged and directed the editorial process, and, with Dorretta D. Stephens, Jackie Hoskins, Mary Morganfield, Tracy D'Almeida, Reba Gales, Sarah Stephens, Bridgette Jackson, and Dwayne Ingram, fine-tuned the manuscript into a book.

To Carla Hayes and Brenda Battle who encouraged and supported me throughout the whole process by serving as great sounding boards as I analyzed each of the sons' secrets.

To Bishop James A. Johnson, my very fine pastor, who has known me all of my life and is responsible for molding my spiritual character. Thank you Bishop Johnson for being a pliable instrument in God's hands to positively affect the lives of others.

To the tribal leaders of the Bethesda Temple Church Men's Ministry, and to Carlton Francis, Isadore Barton, Leroy Long, David Lee, Peter Barnes III, Skip Brown, Sean Brasfield, Rod Byrth, Olufemi Osoko, William Clines, Mickey Flanigan, Dr. Steve Haymon, Julian Johnson, Wilson Meeks, Ardie McCoy, David Patin, Colby Potts, Fred Reed, Tommy Roberston, Carl Solomon, Earl Bingham, Armand Slaughter, Duane Thomas, Craig Fowler and Dr. Johnny James who all loved me, encouraged me and motivated me to apply the tribal concept as we ministered to the needs of people in the St. Louis Metropolitan Area.

Table of Contents

FOREWORD

I am convinced that God has given Ron a gift of understanding and interpretation of the scriptures. Using this gift, he weaves a fascinating tale of a biblical family in *The Power of Secrets*. The result is a new millennium parable. Ron introduces us to one of the poster children of dysfunctional families with secrets: Jacob's two wives, two slave girls, twelve sons, and one daughter. Through Jacob's family, Ron allegorically reveals that most things that happen in Vegas do not stay there and that all of our indiscretions do not stay hidden. In *The Power of Secrets*, Ron outlines the degrees of secrecy (good and bad) and the fallout once they are released. In today's society they could range from life in the ghetto to a victim of incest, an abortion, incarceration or drug addiction. He ministers to women who are rejected by the men they love; abandoned children who struggle in adulthood; and those who carry a list of failures in their lives. Ron reminds us that God has His secrets, too, such as elevating you to become your boss's boss—ah, the sweet revenge of God, restoring your marriage, or healing your body before a doctor could make an incision. The redeeming part in *The Power of Secrets* is the chapter on the Secret Place. It is a spiritual realm where God blocks the devil's aim. After all, in the battlefield, God does not play fair. Let the devil show up with a pistol, God will equip us with our own arsenal of spiritual AK-47s.

Warning: *The Power of Secrets* is a tactical manual for recovering sin addicts, struggling faith seekers, and Christian soldiers who want to memorize God's game plan with scripture-based strategic moves to outwit the enemy in combat.

-Pat Simmons

Pat Simmons is a bestselling and awarding winner author of the Christian romance novels: the Guilty series: *Guilty of Love, Not Guilty of Love, Still Guilty, and Free from Guilt.*

PROLOGUE

I discovered the power of secrets unintentionally. Throughout my twenty-eight years of ministering and counseling, I realized that many people were concealing powerful secrets that dramatically affected their lives. As I counseled, it seemed that women were more ready and willing to share their secrets (making it easier for me to minister/counsel them), but men tended to conceal their secrets under the cloaks of egoism and fear. When I first discovered the power of secrecy, the job appeared to be exclusively for a psychologist or psychiatrist. However, upon closer examination of secrets, I realized that much of the destructive behavior stemmed from spiritual warfare. I was not fighting "flesh and blood" but spirits (Ephesians 6:12). These spirits were driven by invisible demons and generational curses that no psychiatry or psychology could ever solve. Many people do not know that secrets carry spirits. I now understand how the blood of Jesus exposes secret sins (Hebrews 4:13) and removes the "sting of death" (1 Corinthians 15:56).

This book was written for men and women. However, the subject of secrecy helped me to better understand why men struggled with intimacy. Intimacy is the ability to share secrets without being condemned or judged. Many men cannot experience intimacy because they are afraid of the consequences of being exposed. Men who are habitual liars, self-haters, pedophiles, and drug dealers, insecure, boastful, on the down low, suicidal and depressed are often driven by a litany of dark secrets.

All secrets are not bad. Some secrets can empower you while other secrets can stagnate you. More often than not, a large percentage of my counseling time consisted of finding and helping the counselee interpret secret meanings of their circumstances. After I exposed their secrets, I always helped the counselee to redefine and rewrite their history through the death, burial and resurrection of Jesus Christ. During my daily Bible reading, I could not separate the "power of secrecy" from the Holy Scriptures. It became more evident that the power of secrets was an integral theme that ran throughout the Bible. The words secret, secrets, and secretly appear over ninety times in the Bible (KJV).

In the beginning of the Bible, the Book of Genesis, we are told that Eve sinned because the serpent persuaded her that God was keeping a secret from her. At the end of the Bible, in the Book of Revelation, Apostle John received a glimpse of the secrets of the apocalypse, including secrets relating to the mark of the beast. In the Bible there are many stories shrouded with themes of secrecy.

The power of secrets is based on a true story that unveils the secrets of Jacob's dysfunctional family as recorded in Genesis 28 to 49. I chose to write about Jacob's dysfunctional family because they had many family secrets. Each family member personifies a quality. Some are moral qualities such as courage, honesty, and compassion. Some are immoral qualities such as being overly sensual, lazy, lacking self-control, greedy, and slanderous. Whatever the case, my hope is that these moral and practical lessons about secrecy will catapult you to be more like Christ.

I hope this book will liberate everyone, but especially men. This book is about change. It is my goal that you will understand the intricacies of secrets and learn to get rid of the bad secrets and hold on to the good secrets. As you read this book, I hope you will become as fascinated with the power of secrets as I have become.

I hope you will understand the complexity of secrets and the simplicity of the gospel that conquers all secrets. I hope you will be more willing to share your secrets with people whom you can trust. I pray you will cast your secrets upon the Lord because He cares for you (1 Peter 5:7).

When I was a little boy, a preacher visited our church in North St. Louis and told a story that I will never forget. His story was about three pastors who met during the course of a confidential pastoral retreat. The three pastors bonded quickly and decided to take a small fishing boat into the middle of the lake. They enjoyed several hours of fishing, and during the outing, the first pastor decided to confide in the others, saying, "I must confess that the reason I am here is because I have a drinking and a stealing problem. I have been drinking and stealing money from my church for nearly seven years." He then pulled his fishing pole into the boat and began to weep quietly.

The second preacher, gaining courage from the candidness and repentance of the first pastor, said, "The reason I am here is because I am a womanizer and I am addicted to pornography. I have spent hundreds of hours on porno sites on my computer." He dropped his head with embarrassment and further confessed, "I have even had a couple extramarital affairs. God help me!"

At this point, the third pastor could barely stop rocking the boat, feeling the urgent need to confess his own sin. He blurted out, "I do not have a problem with drinking, stealing money, adultery, or pornography," he began. Taking a deep breath, he continued, "but since you two guys have been so open and honest with me, I feel I must share with you my single, secret weakness: I just cannot keep a secret … I just cannot keep my mouth shut … and I just cannot wait to get back home to tell my deacons the mess you guys have gotten yourselves in." The story goes that only two preachers returned from the fishing trip.

Secrets are very powerful. Most psychiatrists, psychologists, and pastors would agree that "you are as sick as your secrets." People who harbor nasty little secrets tend to get infected by those secrets. As genetics and chromosomes are responsible for physical development, so are our secrets responsible for daily behavior. Our secret experiences shape our personalities. Secrecy is the psychological fabric, or the DNA, of personality development. If you want to understand human behavior, then you must understand secret experiences and how they affect and mold lives. They shape the personalities of children and adults. Secrets are like houses where spirits and emotions live. Demons are always looking for ugly secrets to make new homes.

Secrets have voices that will not shut up—they silently whisper to your conscience at will. They even have the ability to torment the mind. Secrets are living, breathing organisms. The law of secrecy states, "The power of a secret is in direct proportion to the consequences of its exposure." For example, if you tell a secret and something really bad or good happens as a result of exposing it, then it is a really powerful secret!

Secrets sell. We are a society mesmerized by secrecy. The word secret has become one of the most popular words of the twenty-first century. It is more popular than communism, capitalism, race relations, education, or religion. If you want to sell a magazine, newspaper, book, or produce a movie, just put secret in the headline or title and watch the product sell. Like Eve in the garden, everyone wants to know more secrets.

Over and over again we purchase and read articles about the secret of losing weight, the secret of becoming a millionaire, the secret of finding a good man, the secret scandals among our political and religious leaders, the secrets of a good sex life, the secret of keeping a woman happy, the secret of getting a reduction on your taxes, the secret lives of movie stars, and so on. The media has invaded our homes with TV talk shows that expose horrific secrets.

Over the last three decades, the media industry has made billions of dollars exposing ugly, dark secrets. We have been inundated with the ugly "tell all" biographies, autobiographies and media feeding frenzies around many politicians and public figures. The old and new TV talk-show hosts such as Joey Greco (best known for hosting the reality TV show Cheaters), Maury Povich (who produced the first maternity test done on National Television), Oprah Winfrey, Jerry Springer, and Montel Williams just to name a few, built their financial empires through the nationwide exposure of secrets. Now, "Reality TV" attempts to expose more secrets.

Unfortunately, audiences love to watch people painfully unveil their secrets through such media outlets. Many of the guests who visit these talk shows are often from super-dysfunctional families … and they tell all! Nothing is revered, and nothing is kept from viewers. The television stations receive high ratings for broadcasting these twisted and perverted secrets. I always feel appalled and angry at their guests who curse their mothers or boast of their perverted love affairs with their parents and children. Exposing secrets is big business. We live in a culture where people are more willing to talk about their sex lives than their prayer lives.

Secrets of the magicians. A magician knows the power of a secret. When everyone in the audience knows how the magician pulls a rabbit from his or her hat the act is no longer magic. Hence, magicians have attempted to unite and develop a code of secrecy. Parts of this code were inspired by the Magician's Code established in 1993 by the International Brotherhood of Magicians and modified for use with the Magic Secrets Network. The magician's code of secrecy is a statement of ethical guidelines designed to help keep the art of magic a secret, alive and healthy, however the code of secrecy is not legally protected. Many TV programs and internet websites continue to reveal the most sacred of magician secrets. Unfortunately, giving away the secrets of how a particular stunt was done, takes the magic out of it.

A secret is anything someone wants to keep hidden from either the view or knowledge of other people. Secrecy is the practice of hiding information from others. No one has divine transparency! Secret thoughts and feelings are a way of life. No one expresses every thought. Hence, everyone has secrets, and even people who say they do not have secrets will invariably reveal deep ones. Yes, we all have secret thoughts. We all have secret lives. Some secrets are hidden in metaphorical closets, in mental cubbyholes, or behind emotional veils.

We all have a tendency of concealing our problems and discontentments. Benjamin Franklin stated that some things should remain secret. He said, "Let thy discontents be thy secrets."

There are many reasons why people keep secrets; let us consider a few:

- they have information that could harm them or you...so they do not want to expose it.

- they do not want to admit to wrongdoing.

- it is a part of their job description.

- they are convinced that it is the path of least resistance.

- they feel fearful about people knowing their secret faults and failures.

- they think people would not like them if they knew everything about them.

- they do not know how to express their feelings - elation, hurt, sadness, love.

- they know that information is power (so they conceal it).

- they do not want to be judged or second-guessed by others.

- they feel no one else can understand why they did what they did.

- they have pledged to keep the matter confidential.

- they are afraid of the consequences and they feel that emotional weight of sharing a secret could cause problems.

- they fear and distrust that other people will not keep their secret.

- the secret has been alive so long that they inherited it.

It is hard to keep a secret. Keeping a secret is a true test of character. Francois Duc de La Rochefoucauld, a French cardinal of the Catholic Church (1558-1645), said, "How can we expect another to keep our secret if we have been unable to keep it ourselves?" Proverbs 11:13 (NIV) states that sharing a secret affects how we relate to each other, "A gossip betrays a confidence, but a trustworthy man keeps a secret."

The world is full of secrets. There are dark secrets, positive and negative secrets, highly classified secrets, medical and legal secrets, family secrets, corporate secrets, theological secrets, etc. Secrets are very powerful. Below are a few characteristics of secrets.

- They are inner-voices that never stop talking.

- They are voices of the subconscious.

- They have the power to separate and unite. They divide families.

- They are like a living organism—images pulsate and pictures flash across our mind.

- They have the power to isolate and alienate.

- They produce energy—and secret energy is transferable. When you tell your secret to someone it releases energy in you (and sometimes this energy is prematurely released). Do not tell your secret too soon.

- They can be cancerous. They grow until they are converted into action.

- If not exposed, they can perpetuate racism and sexism.

- They are the catalyst to lies, liars, and lying. People lie because of the power of fear. Secrecy protects our deceptions and lies. Every liar values secrecy.

- Secrets are the DNA (or deoxyribonucleic acid) that shape personality and define character. How you manage your secrets determines who you are and where you are going.

- They are the cause of divorces and marital failures.

- They are the fabrics that form loyalty and confidence.

- They are leveraging power for any negotiator, lawyer, salesperson, or pastor.

This book analyzes the lives of a dysfunctional family in the Bible who had many secrets. There are many dysfunctional families in the Bible, but Jacob's family was probably the most dysfunctional family in the Bible. The book focuses on Jacob's prophesy concerning his twelve sons. Some of Jacob's sons were murderers, sex offenders, narcissistic, deceivers, and truce breakers, etc. In each chapter, Jacob exposes each of his sons' secrets and prophesied their destiny. Jacob foresaw the secret outcomes of his sons' lives—some were good and others bad. The book is about deliverance and underscores the importance of being open, truthful and honest. You cannot keep secrets from God. In the long run, you will have a better relationship with God and be respected more for your honesty than for your secrecy.

Each chapter reviews the prophecies and secret lives of Jacob's twelve sons beginning with the oldest as found in Genesis 28 through Genesis 49. Each chapter ends with pragmatic Points to Ponder that are designed to inspire readers to better address secret issues in their lives.

Before reading this book, I highly recommend that you read the book of Genesis chapters 27-50. On many occasions, I make references, flashback and flash-forward to scriptures and stories. Your familiarity with the stories will give you a greater appreciation for this book.

Jacob - A Father of Secrets

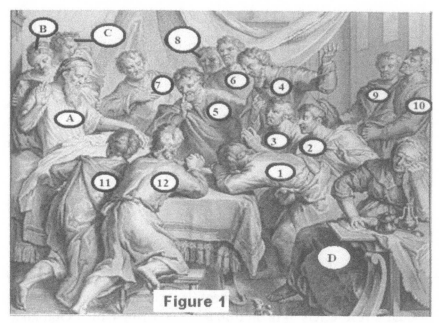

Figure 1 -- *(This image is in courtesy of Bizzell Bible Collection, University of Oklahoma Libraries; copyright the Board of Regents of the University of Oklahoma.)*

1-Reuben; 2-Simeon; 3-Levi; 4-Judah; 5-Dan; 6-Naphtali; 7-Gad; 8-Asher; 9-Issachar; 10-Zebulun; 11-Benjamin; 12-Joseph; A-Jacob; B-Bilhah; C-Zilpah and D-Dinah.

"And Jacob called unto his sons, and said, Gather yourselves together, that I may tell you that which shall befall you in the last days. Gather yourselves together, and hear, ye sons of Jacob; and hearken unto Israel your father" (Genesis 49:1–2).

The above picture shows Jacob's twelve sons, daughter and two concubines. Jacob was old, ready to die, and this was his last message to his twelve sons. It was prophetic because he said, "Gather together, that I may tell you what shall befall you in the last days." In this scene, Jacob called for a conference at his bedside with his twelve sons.

Jacob's sons anxiously surrounded his bed and awaited his prophetic words. Jacob had lived in Egypt for seventeen years. He only had a few hours to live, and it was time for the final blessings to be pronounced upon his sons. The above picture shows Jacob lying on his deathbed (identified by the letter "A"). The picture depicts the entire family surrounding Jacob with great anticipation and excitement. Bilhah and Zilpah, his concubines are standing directly behind him and appear to prop him up so he can speak with his sons (characters B and C). He was weak, blind, and 147 years old. At that age he was ready to speak with each of his sons and prophesy concerning their future.

Yes, Jacob was about to reveal his boys' secrets. They had questions—lots of questions—like, "Which family will produce a judge?", "Which family will produce a king?", "Which family will produce a prophet?", "Which family will have the most land?", "Which family will be the greatest?", and "Which family will be the richest?" It was an exciting moment. It was a fearful moment. God would reveal secrets to them through their dying father! God knew the secrets of their future!

Jacob was a man of faith (Hebrews 11:20), and this pronouncement of blessings was an act of faith because up to this point his sons had not developed into tribes.

According to *New Unger's Bible Dictionary*, prophesy is when a person "tells forth" or "predicts what God is going to do before it occurs." Nobody can accurately foretell the future unless God informs him or her of it. God spoke to Jacob, and Jacob decided he would reveal secrets concerning each son's destiny—they would become the founding fathers of the nation of Israel.

But before we deal with the secrets of the first son, let us turn our attention to Jacob and his secrets.

For twenty years, Rebekah and Isaac had no children (Genesis 25:20, 26). God told Rebekah that she would have twins but they would

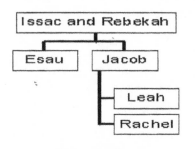

Figure 2

have very different personalities. They would go their separate ways and father two different nations. The oldest son would be stronger but would serve his younger brother. In other words, the destiny of the family would be passed on to the second-born child.

The first son was covered with red hair, so he was named Esau, which means, "hairy." The second son was born holding onto his brother's heel, so they named him Jacob. Jacob means "heel-catcher, supplanter, one who takes the place of another by treachery or trickery." Jacob's name was prophetic of how he behaved later in life.

Blessings versus birthright. The right to lead the family is generally referred to as "the blessing" and is not to be confused with the birthright. The birthright was a double portion of the inheritance when the father died. The general practice was for the blessing to go to the first-born son, but this did not happen in the case of Esau and Jacob. Isaac was aware of God's choice. Over time, however, he began to favor his eldest son, Esau.

Esau's secret issues. As he and his brother grew, Esau learned the secrets of hunting. He became an outdoorsman and a noted hunter. While he hunted in the field he met many attractive women. Esau had two weaknesses—sleeping with the ungodly women and frequent cursing (Hebrews 12:16). Esau's secret lust for women and secret (curse) words were toxic and the cause of his downfall.

Jacob's secret issues. Unlike his brother (Esau), Jacob learned the secrets of domestication. He stayed close to home and is described as a plain or peaceable man. Jacob was a mama's boy—he was tied to Rebekah's apron strings.

As a young man, Jacob lived a life of secrecy. Many secret issues plagued his life, and they are listed below.

1. He was a con man. He coerced Esau into selling his birthright (Genesis 25:30, 31).

2. He was a thief and a liar. He stole Esau's blessing (Genesis 27:30).

3. He lacked honor and integrity. He was crafty and deceitful. He pretended to be Esau (Genesis 27:32).

4. He violated his conscience and tricked his blind father (Genesis 27:1).

5. He was inconsistent. He displayed acts of spirituality and then acts of carnality.

6. He was selfish and would not give his brother food without bargaining over it (Genesis 25:33, 34).

7. He was a victim of his mother's partiality. Rebekah secretly loved Jacob more than Esau (Genesis 25:28).

8. He blasphemed the name of the Lord. (Genesis 27:20).

CHAPTER 1

THE SECRET OF REUBEN

SEXUAL SECRETS

"Unstable as water, thou shalt not excel; because thou wentest up to thy father's bed; then defiledst thou it: he went up to my couch" (Genesis 49:4).

Sex is powerful. Sexual secrets are even more powerful. Do you have a sexual secret? Whether you have a strong sexual appetite or no sex drive at all, sex is what makes the world go around. The human sex drive is like a magnet—it attracts people, pleasure, and problems. Sexual issues and problems are everywhere and will continue to mount. Like the Roman Empire, America will decline because of her people's sexual promiscuity.[1] Roman historians recount "there

---

[1]   *Cullen Murphy, Are we Rome? Houghton Mifflin, May 2008*

were 32,000 prostitutes in Rome during the reign of Roman Emperor Trajan.

America's demise will be the consequences of pornography. The insatiable thirst for sex will weaken America. Pornography and a new sexual revolution will thrive in the name of freedom of the press. Pedophiles and child pornographers will secretly thrive on the Internet,[2] and millions of people will continue to purchase pornographic magazines, videotapes, DVDs, and start new porno Web sites. Legislation will redefine marriage, and same-sex marriages will soon become old news.

Sexual secrets are uncovered every day, yet millions of people are still hiding in the closet. The term "on the down-low" is no longer a new term for homosexuals who conceal their bi-sexual relationships. But as the Bible declared every secret (good or bad) will be exposed (Ecclesiastes 12:14).

Even as I write this chapter, secrets are being exposed. Many of our American Catholic priests are pleading guilty to sexual crimes committed against our innocent children. Also, American Protestant pastors and preachers are being caught in adulterous relationships, and politicians are being caught and charged with sexual improprieties. Even some of our school teachers are being charged with soliciting sex from their young students. God help us!

Viagra and sex toys are topping the market in sales. Geneticists are feverishly searching DNA structures in hope of discovering the gene that determines sexual orientation. Men study genetics, but God knows the heart. "Shall not God search this out? for he knoweth the secrets of the heart" (Psalm 44:21). The Bible made it plain when it stated that no secret work could be hidden. The psalmist declared that every secret sin would be exposed. He wrote, "Thou hast set our iniquities before thee, our secret sins in the light of thy countenance" (Psalm 90:8). Apostle Paul wrote to the Church about secrets. He said, "In the day when God shall judge the secrets of men by Jesus Christ according to my gospel" (Romans 2:16). You must get rid of ugly secrets.

---

[2]   *Phillip Jenkins, Beyond Tolerance: Child Pornography on the Internet (New York University Press, 2001)*

In this chapter we will consider Reuben's sexual secrets and the factors which exposed his sexual promiscuity. As we analyze the sexual secrets of Reuben, we will consider the following factors:

1) Reuben's inability to excel
2) Reuben's instability
3) His mandrakes and early sex education
4) His incestuous relationship with Bilhah
5) The secret addiction to pornography
6) Overcoming sexual secrets

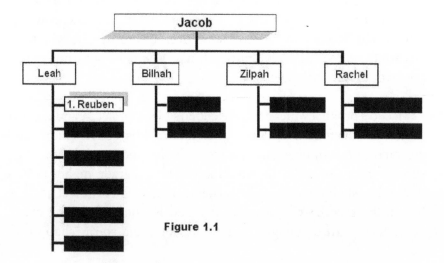

Figure 1.1

Each of Jacob's sons was faced with a challenge, and Reuben was the one most predisposed to a sexual addiction. Let us review the reasons for Reuben's sexual disposition. Reuben disappeared when Joseph needed him the most, leading Jacob to establish that Reuben was unstable as water. So, I suggest that his sexual instability caused Reuben to disappear at a defining moment in his life. As far as sexual instability, Reuben is sexually informed as a young child. He found mandrakes, an ingredient for a sexual love potion, for his mother. Later in his life, he went to bed with Bilhah and possible raped her. Reuben's family was the first family to fall to apostasy (departure from God). Let us look closer at the sexual secrets of Reuben.

1) Reuben's inability to excel. In Genesis 49:1–2, twelve bearded sons are called together to receive prophetic words from their father before he dies. Jacob predicted how his sons' lives would unfold. His predictions were based on revelations from God, which were insights to the consequences of their behavior. He began with his firstborn son, Reuben. Jacob prophesized that Reuben "shalt not excel." This meant the birthright would be taken from Reuben and given to another brother. *Webster's Dictionary* defines excel as, "to be superior; to surpass in accomplishment or achievement; to surpass others." This meant that Reuben would never surpass his brothers, and he would never be given a leadership role. So, Reuben lost his kingship, which would be given to Judah, his priestly call, which would be given to his brother Levi, and his prophetic provocation—Joseph would inherit that. Reuben lost his influence over his brothers, to which his birthright at one time had entitled him. When he spoke unto them they would not hear (Genesis 42:22).

Jacob's prophecy meant that Reuben's ideas, projects, and dreams would be incomplete and below standard. His conversations and personal interactions would always be faulty and second-rate. If he enrolled in a university he would never earn a grade higher than a "C," as he "shall not excel." An unstable man can never excel because his thinking is flawed. Jacob condemned Reuben to mediocrity, to never have a great thought! His mind, soul, and spirit "shall never excel."

It was painful for Jacob to utter such a negative prophecy concerning his son because when Reuben was born, Jacob had big dreams for him. Reuben was Jacob's pride and joy. In Genesis 49:3, Jacob declared five things about Reuben. He called Reuben:

- "my firstborn"

- "my might"

- "the beginning of my strength"

- "the excellency of dignity"

- "the excellency of power"

As Jacob's firstborn, Reuben was destined to receive his father's inheritance and excel beyond his brothers. Genesis 49:3 tells us of Jacob's wonderful expectation. However, the next verse tells us of Jacob's great disappointment. Jacob declared, "Unstable as water, thou shalt not excel; because thou wentest up to thy father's bed; then defiledst thou it: he went up to my couch" (Genesis 49:4). The phrase "went into his father's bed" refers to an adulterous relationship. Reuben was disqualified from his position as eldest son when he committed an act of sexual immorality with Jacob's concubine Bilhah (Genesis 35:22). Because of Reuben's unstable, secret sex life, he lost it all! How many pastors, politicians, leaders, spouses, and friends have lost it all because of a secret sexual experience that was exposed?

Reuben never received a second opportunity to excel—his act was too egregious. However, there are many people in the Bible with unstable personality traits who went on to excel in life. Here are a few examples:

- Moses is seen as an unstable and insecure man, whom the anger of the Lord was kindled against, however, Exodus 4:13 says, "And he said, O my Lord, send, I pray thee, by the hand of him whom thou wilt send." Moses then goes on to excel as one of Israel's greatest leaders.

- Jonah, the rebellious evangelist, demonstrated instability when he attempted to escape the presence of God. He later went on to conduct one of the greatest revivals in Nineveh.

- Hezekiah displayed instability when he allowed the Babylonians to enter the Holy Temple (2 Kings 20:15). Hezekiah did a terrible thing. God said he would kill Hezekiah for this encroachment (Isaiah 38:1), but

Hezekiah wept and repented (Isaiah 38:2–4). The death sentence was cancelled and God allowed Hezekiah to live another fifteen years (Isaiah 38:5).

• Mary Magdalene was a prostitute. Her life was unstable. She met Jesus and he changed her life. She excelled to become one of the first female evangelists. Her first sermon was entitled, "Come, see a man!" (John 4:29).

• In Luke 15, the prodigal son left home, lost all of his wealth through his irresponsibility and instability, but returned to his father, repented, and excelled.

A family waiting to excel. Reuben's family grew to become a large tribe (Numbers 1:21), but they never excelled. As far as we know, neither a prophet, nor a judge, nor a king ever came out of the tribe of Reuben. After coming out of Egypt, Reuben was the first tribe assigned to the Promised Land and the first tribe to be removed by the enemy. God stirred up the spirits of the kings of Assyria (1 Chronicles 5:18–26) and destroyed the family of Reuben, quickly proving Jacob's prophecy true.

In Genesis 37, Reuben's nine brothers (Benjamin was not yet born) developed a scheme to kill Joseph. Jacob's sons hated Joseph because he was the firstborn son of Rachel, Jacob's preeminent wife at the time. This firstborn position entitled Joseph to distinguished favors, which were conferred upon Joseph in many ways. Jacob gave Joseph a coat of many colors because of his special love for him. Because of his father's special love, Reuben clearly displays his hate of his brother Joseph.

It is Satan who inspired Jacob's sons to hate Joseph. Their hatred was so intense that they plotted to murder Joseph, saying, "Come, and let us slay him" (Genesis 37:20). His brothers were murderers. 1 John 3:15 says, "Whosoever hateth his brother is a murderer ...."

A time to excel. Reuben opposed his brothers' plot to murder Joseph. "And Reuben said unto them, 'Shed no blood, but cast him into this pit that is in the wilderness, and lay no hand upon him; that he might rid him out of their hands, to deliver him to his father again'" (Genesis 37:22). Quite naturally, as the eldest son, Reuben should have protested against any scheme against his brother. Reuben should have said, "Not over my dead body will you hurt my little brother or throw him in a pit." Reuben compromised to a lesser evil. "Do not kill him," he shouted, "throw him in the pit instead." Reuben's suggestion pacified the anger of his nine brothers, and he even appeared sympathetic. He showed a (temporary) sign of being a real hero. Reuben planned to rescue Joseph from the pit after his angry brothers left the scene. Yet, although his brothers agreed not to kill their little brother, Reuben is only partially successful because his little secret plan to rescue Joseph from the pit failed. The specific responsibility of the firstborn was to come to the aid of any family member who gets into trouble. Reuben failed to exercise his authority and failed in his responsibility of saving Joseph (Genesis 37:21-30).

Reuben's failure to rescue his brother was a defining moment. A defining moment is a time in our lives in which we make a quality decision that elevates us and defines our character. A defining moment is a chance to make a quality mark on the world for which people will remember us. Reuben failed to return his brother to his father's hand, and it was an early sign to Jacob that Reuben "shall not excel." You cannot excel if you miss the opportunity to excel.

Another missed opportunity to excel. Reuben mysteriously disappeared after he persuaded his angry brothers not to kill Joseph. Reuben's disappearance is quite puzzling. Why did Reuben disappear after he stopped his brothers from killing Joseph? Was the situation too stressful? Where did Reuben go? Did he go to a prostitute's house in Dothan? Did he visit a girlfriend's home nearby? Did he have a secret male companion nearby? It is uncertain where Reuben went or for how long he was away from the wilderness, but when Reuben returned to the pit to rescue Joseph, he learned that Joseph had been sold into slavery by his nine brothers for twenty pieces of silver. Why didn't Reuben pursue the slave-buyers and rescue Joseph? Was he too frightened to demand the silver back from his riotous brothers in exchange for his brother? Whatever the reason, Reuben failed to excel and was uncertain where he should go after this debacle.

Oscar nomination or "whither shall I go"? When Reuben learned that Joseph had been sold into slavery, he could have won an Oscar Award. He shouted, screamed, rolled around in the rocky, desert wilderness, and tore his garments apart. Reuben's anguish was not for Joseph's whereabouts but for his own skin. "The child is not, whither shall I go?" (Genesis 37:30). Reuben was frightened to face the wrath of Jacob. Sometimes our tears are selfish. We fear consequences and we weep for ourselves and not for the loved ones who are gone.

Elimination of competition. As the eldest son, Reuben was entitled to inherit Jacob's kingship, his priesthood, and his prophet's mantle. However, he feared his irresponsibility would cause him to forfeit these birthright privileges. However, with Joseph (the firstborn of Rachel) now eliminated, Reuben might have thought he had a better chance of winning the birthright privileges.

Joseph's disappearance remained a secret. The sons of Jacob (including Reuben) agreed to keep the disappearance of Joseph a secret. They tore Joseph's coat, killed a kid (a young goat), soaked the coat in blood, and began a brutal campaign of secrecy that continued for more than twenty years. Joseph's disappearance remained a secret until his brothers journeyed to Egypt, where a renewed Joseph asked the question, "Have ye a father?" (Genesis 44:19).

Two missed opportunities to be heroic. During the years of famine, as the sons of Jacob traveled back and forth between Egypt and Canaan, Simeon was held captive in Egypt until the sons of Israel brought their youngest brother Benjamin to Egypt. Reuben had the opportunity to take the place of Simeon. He could have said no, "I will stay as a hostage, but let my little brother Simeon return home. But, fearing for his life in Egypt, Reuben failed to take Simeon's place (Genesis 42:18-24). Secondly, Reuben failed to take responsibility for Benjamin. It was Judah who promised his father that he would take full responsibility for Benjamin (Genesis 43:9). Reuben could have said, "Dad, as the oldest son I will ensure Benjamin's safety." He allowed Judah to do what he should have done as the firstborn (Genesis 43:1-9). Here, Reuben missed two opportunities to be valiant.

2) Reuben's instability. Jacob declared Reuben to be "unstable as water." Water has interesting characteristics—it has no shape or foundation, it evaporates and is unsteady, when spilled it cannot be picked up or recovered, it is unpredictable, it leaves no trail when ships sail over it, when spilled it follows the course of least resistance, it attracts mosquitoes, and it smells if it sits too long. Reuben's future is compared to boiling, unstable water.

In the Scriptures, we see Reuben as a young boy raised up in a perverted, chaotic, and unstable environment. Reuben knew that his family was quite dysfunctional—his mother (Leah) was a puppet who was controlled by her father (Laban) and married through a fraudulent process, his father (Jacob) was a deceiver, his uncle (Esau) wanted to kill his father, and his grandfather (Laban) was conniving. Everything about Reuben's life was unstable. Men who are unstable are dangerous!

An unstable thought-life is the root cause of sexual promiscuity. Bestiality, homosexuality, adultery, fornication, and other such behaviors are all symptoms of a perverted sexual thought-life. If you can control your thought-life you can control your sex life. However, it is very difficult to find information (in books, on the Internet, etc.) on how to control your sexual thought-life. Jesus, though, speaks clearly on controlling your sexual thought-life (Matthew 5:28), telling us that perverted thinking always leads to perverted behavior. The most powerful tool in the world is your thought-life.

So, just as water takes the shape of its container, Reuben's thought-life took the shape of his perverted and chaotic environment. His thought-life was "as unstable as water." It is double mindedness that opens the door to pornography, incest, and the like. James 1:8 says, "A double minded man is unstable in all his ways."

Emotional turmoil. Reuben's environment was full of emotional turmoil. His father rejected Reuben's mother, and his father was tricked into marrying his mother (Genesis 29:31–34). Leah felt intense rejection and isolation, but when Reuben was born she declared that her son was born to alleviate her afflictions and feelings of rejection. Leah had been emotionally distraught and neglected by Jacob's hatred, but then she was given the most precious gift a woman could receive—a baby. "And Leah conceived, and bare a son, and she called his name Reuben: for she said, 'Surely the LORD hath looked upon my affliction'" (Genesis 29:32). Leah believed that giving birth to a baby would cause Jacob to love her.

A baby in exchange for love. After giving birth, she said, "Now therefore my husband will love me" (Genesis 29:32). The overwhelming feeling of love and generosity from God not only opened her womb but also rekindled her lost soul. Leah now had a new focus and promise in her life. Her child would love her and Jacob could not take that away. This gift temporarily subdued her pain of rejection. Would the new baby force Jacob to see Leah differently and cause him to love her, or would the new baby increase his resentment, knowing that the woman he truly loved could not conceive?

How often do we lose our patience, while hunting for gratification, and take matters into our own hands? Women are capable of becoming pregnant through secret manipulation. Some are desperately seeking affection, emotionally and physically, and feel they must use a child to accomplish that end. Does this deception provide the cure for their pain? Certainly not, for this often causes more hatred and deception, and it is made worse because now there is an innocent child involved.

Unstable fathers produce unstable sons. Reuben was raised in an environment absent of love. His home was cold, void of affection, and "as unstable as water." He never heard his dad call his mom "sweetheart," "baby," "darling," or "honey." In fact, the Bible says Jacob hated his wife (Genesis 29:31). Did Reuben learn how to hate from his father? A father's role in a home is to set the atmosphere. An ungodly father creates an ungodly atmosphere in his home. A godly father creates a godly atmosphere. Fathers cannot predict the future for their families, but they can create a path for the future by controlling the family atmosphere. Jacob's lethargic, ambivalent feelings toward Leah fostered an unhealthy and unstable family atmosphere. The best gift a father can give his children is to love their mother. Reuben never received this gift. The instability of Reuben was a consequence of his loveless family-atmosphere.

3) His mandrakes and early sex education. "And Reuben went in the days of wheat harvest, and found mandrakes in the field, and brought them unto his mother Leah. Then Rachel said to Leah, 'Give me, I pray thee, of thy son's mandrakes'" (Genesis 30:14).

Figure 1.2

Another sign of Reuben's sexual secret is his knowledge and access to mandrakes. Mandrakes are plant roots believed to promote fertility. As shown in Figure 1.2, the shape of the root resembles the waist and thighs of a man or woman in that its thick root is often forked, suggesting human legs, and it frequently has additional side roots which appear like arms. This resemblance has led to many superstitions associated with the mandrake. Reuben, at age six or seven, is well educated about sex. He knows that his mom (Leah) and aunt (Rachel) are competing to have babies with Jacob. Genesis 30:14 tells us that Reuben finds mandrakes during the harvest. Reuben's discovery of mandrakes in the field is equivalent to a son who returns home with Viagra for his father. The fact that Reuben knew where to locate the mandrakes and how they were used suggests that Reuben received early sex education (Genesis 30:14). Who taught Reuben about the mandrake and its fertility secrets? Did the boys on the street teach him about sex?

The secret power of mandrakes. The word "mandrake" is only mentioned twice in the Bible (Genesis 30 and Song of Solomon 7). In Song of Solomon 7:13, mandrakes are noted for their pleasant, sexual odor. Mandrakes are leafy plants eaten by women with the belief that this would aid them in becoming pregnant. The fruit of the mandrake, according to ancient texts, is a species of melon of a most agreeable odor. According to the *World Book Encyclopedia*, mandrakes, when ripe, are the size and color of a small apple—exceedingly ruddy—and although bland tasting and slightly poisonous, they are much desired as an edible fruit. They have been called "Love Apples," as the plant was and still is believed to be an aphrodisiac (a substance that induces or causes one to desire sex) when properly prepared. It was the belief that both the fruit and the root of mandrakes would cause, through magical properties, the fertility and conception of a child for Rachel, and that was what caused her to ask for them.

Desperate housewives. Leah and Rachel were desperate housewives. Leah was desperate to have another baby boy for her husband, but Rachel was even more desperate. Desperate women are dangerous because desperation creates envy. Both wives were envious of each other. Rachel was envious because of Leah's children, and Leah was envious because Rachel had mysteriously won Jacob's love. Why did Jacob love Rachel so deeply? Jacob would always have a certain degree of hate for Leah because he saw her as the object that kept him from his true love, Rachel. Leah was jealous at how much Jacob loved Rachel. Jealousy will cause you to do strange things. The sisters fought over Jacob. Leah screamed to Rachel, "Is it a small matter that thou hast taken my husband?..." (Genesis 30:15).

Superstitious secrets. Leah asked Rachel, "And wouldest thou take away my son's mandrakes also?" (Genesis 30:15). Leah tells Rachel that since she stole Jacob, she could not have the magical mandrakes that would help her have the child she wanted so badly. Believing her fertility would increase if she ate mandrakes, Rachel then offers to pay a price for the mandrakes. Leah agrees to sell her the mandrakes and accepts the price offered. The Bible shows us here the foolishness of believing in and relying on superstitions and magic, as Rachel did not become pregnant after eating the fruit of the mandrake.

4) His incestuous relationship with Bilhah. A key sign of Reuben's instability was his secret, incestuous relationship with Bilhah, his father's maid and concubine, which appears in Genesis 35:22. Perhaps this was a case of rape and incest. *Webster's Dictionary* defines incest as sexual intercourse between persons so closely related that they are forbidden by law to marry. In the secret of the night, Reuben had sexual intercourse with Bilhah. Reuben was caught and will never be forgiven by Jacob for this sin. Proverbs 6:27–29 says: "Can a man take fire in his bosom, and his clothes not be burned? Can one go upon hot coals, and his feet not be burned? So he that goeth in to his neighbor's wife; whosoever toucheth her shall not be innocent."

This is the first biblical account of an incestuous relationship between a son and a mother (or step-mother). Having intercourse with another man's concubine was seen as a deliberate challenge to the other man's power and authority. There are several cases, however, of biblical personalities having sexual intercourse with other men's concubines:

- David's son Absalom, as an act of political rebellion, had sex with ten of his father's concubine "....in the sight of all Israel." (2 Samuel 16:22).

- When the Israelite king, Ishbosheth, accused Abner, his military commander, of "going into" the royal concubine Rizpah. Abner, without denying the charge, became so indignant over being charged ("Am I a dog's head of Judah?") that he switched allegiance, joining David who was King of Judah. (2 Samuel 3:7–12, 4:5–8).

- King Solomon executed his brother, Adonijah, for having the nerve to ask for the royal concubine Abishag the Shunammite in marriage (1 Kings 2:13–25).

Despite his anger, Jacob remained silent for forty years. Only on his deathbed did he finally express his anger about the act. Jacob was old and blind, but he remembered Reuben's indiscretion as he revealed his sons' prophecies. It may have been a surprise to the family.

Reuben's sexual relationship with Bilhah would never be of true love and his need would never be fulfilled. The love he desired was from the love he hadn't received from his own father. He could not replace that with women or action, no matter what levels he resorted to. Through unattainable means, Reuben was trying to fill a secret void in his life. Sexual situations with various women were his attempt to resolve the pain he felt inside. It all began with one lie, one deception, and one greedy little secret.

5) The secret addiction to pornography. For the reasons listed above, I believe Reuben had a secret addiction. According to *Webster's Dictionary*, an addiction is "a repetitive performance of a behavior that appears to be outside of a person's control, despite possible or actual negative consequences." Sexual addiction, however, thrives in secrecy more than any other addiction. As with sexual addiction, pornography addiction is rarely caused by only one factor, but is more likely a building up of conditions over time. Causes for pornographic addiction could include exposure to pornographic images at a young age, deep seated insecurity and/or fear of rejection, or past trauma such as physical and/or sexual abuse.

In addition to these causes, pornographic addictions feed on itself, and are progressive in nature. A person becomes desensitized to the images that are being seen, and constantly needs more new images. In addition, once exposed to more graphic depictions of sexual activity, simple nudity is no longer as exciting. In some cases, this progression into harder pornography can lead to illegal activities such as child pornography.

6) Overcoming sexual secrets. People pay thousands of dollars to psychologists to rid themselves of ugly and dark secrets. The framework in which I am presenting sexual secrets includes: reported and unreported rape and incest; fornication; child pornography; and other sexual perversions. Below, I offer a few suggestions on overcoming secret sexual addictions.

- **Expose the secret to God**. Tell God about your sexual secret. Do not allow the secret to cripple you for the rest of your life. Speak openly but privately to God. If the secret relates to sexual abuse, forgive the person who abused you and ask God to help you release the pain, anger, and guilt that you feel. "Casting all your cares upon him; for he careth for you" (1 Peter 5:7). (If you are aware that the sex offender is still abusing others, then you should report him or her to the local law authorities.)

- **Expose the secret to your pastor**. Tell your sexual secrets to a qualified pastor or professional Christian counselor. Use discretion in telling your sexual secrets to your friends or relatives as they may not be capable of advising or providing you with good counsel.

- **Stop worrying by reading Philippians 4:6–7**. Admit openly but in private that without Jesus Christ in your life you are powerless to overcome the pain of your sexual secrets. Learn the following verse by heart and repeat it each time sexual secrets plague you: "Do not be anxious about anything, but in everything, by prayer and petition, with thanksgiving, present your requests to God. And the peace of God, which transcends all understanding, will guard your hearts and your minds in Christ Jesus" (Philippians 4:6–7 NIV).

- **Sanctify yourself.** Sanctify means to be set apart for God's purpose. You must set yourself apart from anything that is not Christ-like. Destroy any pornographic movies, magazines, or nude pics on your computer. Cut off the Internet and cable television that brings pornography into your home or call the providers and tell them to disconnect X-rated websites and cable stations.

- **"Hate the sin, love the sinner."** If ugly and dark sexual secrets continue to plague your mind, do not start hating yourself. The devil uses self-hatred as a tool for inspiring depression. Love God and yourself, but hate the sin. Do not let your sex drive and sexual secret control your life. Let the Word of God regulate your thoughts.

- **Fight back with a greater image.** Each time a sexual secret or pornographic image comes to mind, challenge it with a greater image. Call on Jesus and pray for the person you see in the image. Ask God to deliver and save the person you see in each mental image.

- **Get yourself a rabbi.** The word, "rabbi" means teacher. Your teacher could be a weekly Bible class, Sunday school class, prayer meeting, course in a Bible college, or study group. The key point is to keep yourself in the presence of "the hearing of the Word."

POINTS TO PONDER

The Secret of Reuben—Sexual Secrets. Reuben was Jacob's first son. His name means to "see a son". His mother's name was Leah. Reuben is symbolic of people with sexual secrets and represents unstable people who cannot control their sexual appetites. Sexual secrets are powerful! The pain and embarrassment of sexual secrets have destroyed many lives. Our world has been plagued by sexual secrets in preachers, politicians, high school principals, and prostitutes. Do you have a sexual secret? Do you know someone on the "down-low"? Sexual predators thrive on secrecy. Victims of sexual abuse and their attackers often conceal sex crimes such as rape, child molestation, or sexual abuse. Jesus warned us about controlling our secret sexual thoughts. Watching pornography on the Internet is one of our nation's darkest secrets. Jacob cursed Reuben for his sexual encroachment and instability. Jacob prophesied that Reuben and his family would be "as unstable as water."

- An unstable thought-life is the root cause of sexual promiscuity.

- If you can control your thought-life you can control your sex life.

- The most powerful tool in the world is your thought-life.

- Men study genetics, but God knows the heart.

- An unstable man can never excel because his thinking is flawed.

- People who are unstable can be compared to boiling, unstable water. Water has no shape or foundation, it evaporates and is unsteady, when spilled it cannot be picked-up or recovered.

- As water takes the shape of its container, Reuben's thought-life took the shape of his environment.

- A father's role in a home is to set the atmosphere for his home. An ungodly father creates an ungodly atmosphere.

- The best gift a father can give his children is to love their mother. Reuben never received this gift.

Reuben lost his birthright and blessing because of sexual indiscretion. However, his eavesdropping brother, Simeon, was more complex and homicidal about the secret things he overheard. Let us take a closer look at Simeon, the eavesdropper.

CHAPTER 2

THE SECRET OF SIMEON

EAVESDROPPING

"Do not eavesdrop on others—you may hear your servant laughing at you" (Ecclesiastes 7:21 NLT).

Eavesdropping is big business. Eavesdropping is an intentional act of secretly listening to a private or confidential conversation. Corporations hire people to eavesdrop and then lure employees from their competitors who are willing to trade inside secrets. More and more businesses are using sophisticated electronic equipment and devices to record confidential discussions. Small groups of eavesdroppers are currently listening (everywhere) for chatter and evidence of terrorist plots. Since the assaults of September 11, 2001 and the continued efforts of Al Qaeda terrorists, the United States government has set a goal of hiring a sufficient number of eavesdroppers to abort any terrorist attacks.

Eavesdropping includes secretly tracking anyone's public movements with a GPS (Global Positioning System) device. Across the nation, investigators and governmental officials are using GPS to catch drug dealers, burglars, stalkers and other criminals. Privacy advocates and criminal defense lawyers who monitor eavesdropping efforts are challenging the usage of GPS. They say the technology goes beyond surveillance and could be used to create a detailed, around-the-clock profile of one's movements. Because the trackers are so affordable, they view them as a privacy threat that could reveal one's political, religious and personal associations to law enforcement. Courts are now grappling with how to balance privacy rights against an investigative technique hailed by state and local police, the Drug Enforcement Administration and FBI. New federal and state laws have been passed to support all legalized forms of governmental eavesdropping.

Unlike, the there presently is a greater need to listen and record private conversations. Nothing is sacred any more. Our cellular phones, computers, televisions and radios, offices and cars, and even our bedroom conversations are all vulnerable to unwanted surveillance. The problems with eavesdroppers are that they often hear only small portions of conversations and reach faulty conclusions. They frequently mislead and misquote people and disseminate incorrect information.

There is an important difference between simply overhearing a conversation and eavesdropping. Eavesdropping is an intentional act of secretly listening to someone else's conversation.

In this chapter, I will consider Simeon who represents the power of eavesdropping.

1) Eavesdroppers in the Bible
2) Jehovah the Eavesdropper
3) The eavesdropping fetus
4) Instruments of cruelty

5) Be angry, but do not sin

6) Warning signs of eavesdropping or bugging

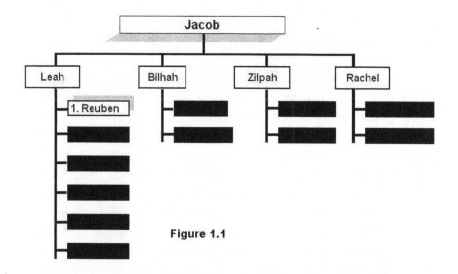

Figure 1.1

People who eavesdrop seek to hear confidential information for the purpose of gossip or personal gain. Eavesdropping means to overhear, record, amplify or transmit any part of the private discourse of others without the permission of all persons engaged in the discourse. There are many examples of people in the Bible who listened to private conservations without the permission of the person who was speaking.

1) Eavesdroppers in the Bible.

- Rebecca eavesdropped when she secretly overheard the conversation between Issac and Esau regarding the blessing Issac intended to give Esau. (Genesis 27:5).

- An unidentified man overheard the ten sons of Jacob say, "Let us go down to Dothan" (Genesis 37:17).

- An Israelite soldier overheard David's testimony of killing a lion and a bear and reported it to King Saul. King Saul then called David for a personal interview (1 Samuel 17:31).

• Elijah overheard the secret military conversations of the King of Moab (2 Kings 6:12).

• Mordecai eavesdropped as he was sitting at the king's gate. He overheard Bigthana and Teresh, two of the king's officers who guarded the doorway, speak angrily and conspire to assassinate King Xerxes (Esther 2:21).

• Gideon and his servant Purah eavesdropped when they snuck into the enemy's camp (Midianites and Amalekites). They overheard a private conversation between two men. One man was telling a friend his dream of being defeated by Gideon. When Gideon heard the private conversation he quietly worshipped and his fear dissipated (Judges 7:10–15).

• Joseph eavesdropped on his brothers. We find in Scripture that Joseph's brothers assumed that the Egyptian viceroy (actually Joseph himself) spoke no Hebrew and took advantage of this fact to hold a private conversation in his presence (Genesis 42:23).

• Doeg the Edomite was eavesdropping when he reported David's plan to King Saul (1 Samuel 22:22).

"Tell no man." On many occasions when Jesus healed someone or performed a miracle he charged the person to keep his identity a secret.

Jesus charged them to tell no man because the time had not yet come for his glory. A premature glory would merely perplex the people, turn their attention away from his words, and keep them from believing in him. The disciples were not yet sufficiently grounded in the truth and would not be so until after Jesus' death and resurrection and the outpouring of the Holy Spirit. Below are a few examples where Jesus said, "tell no man."

- **A man healed from leprosy.** "And Jesus saith unto him, See thou *tell no man*; but go thy way, shew thyself to the priest, and offer the gift that Moses commanded, for a testimony unto them" (Matthew 8:4).

- **A revelation of Christ's God-like character.** "Then charged he his disciples that they should *tell no man* that he was Jesus the Christ" (Matthew 16:20).

- **A man who was healed from being deaf.** "And he charged them that they should *tell no man*: but the more he charged them, so much the more a great deal they published it" (Mark 7:36).

- **The Transfiguration of Jesus.** "And as they came down from the mountain, he charged them that they should *tell no man* what things they had seen, till the Son of man were risen from the dead" (Mark 9:9).

- **A man covered with leprosy.** "And he charged him to *tell no man*: but go, and shew thyself to the priest, and offer for thy cleansing, according as Moses commanded, for a testimony unto them" (Luke 5:14).

- **Jairus' daughter: dead but raised to live again**. "And her parents were astonished: but he charged them that they should *tell no man* what was done" (Luke 8:56).

2) Jehovah the Eavesdropper. Leah believed that God was secretly listening to all of the conversations relating to her rejection. Leah said the Lord had given her a son because he "heard that I was hated" (Genesis 29:33). She felt that God was eavesdropping. I believe Leah was saying, "God has heard the cruelty of my husband. God has heard of the coldness of my husband. God has heard my pain but has blessed me with a second son." Figure 2.1 shows the expanded family tree. Leah believed her pregnancy was an answer from God.

Leah and her son overheard many unpleasant conversations. Jacob's anger and hatred, combined with their deception of eavesdropping and devious planning, could have stockpiled enough pain for life. Leah desperately wanted to win the love of her husband, but she could not get Jacob to listen. Still, she hoped that the birth of a second son would pacify Jacob's anger and turn his ambivalence into love. Every wife wants a husband who will listen. In Genesis 29:33, she rejoiced because God had listened. But her son entered into the world as an angry baby.

Leah's unrealistic hope. Leah hoped to win Jacob's love by giving him another son. She possessed a true love for Jacob but an unrealistic hope for a lasting relationship. The name Leah means, "weary." She was weary of Jacob's rejection, weary of her sister, weary of her father, and weary of herself, but she hoped that Jacob would one day love her. Hope overcame her weariness. The Bible described Leah as ugly and unattractive by using the phrase, "weak eyes." "Leah had weak eyes, but Rachel was lovely in form, and beautiful" (Genesis 29:17 NIV).

Dealing with rejection. When confronted with rejection, many women react the same way as Leah—they attempt to secretly buy the love of their husband. Pregnancy is the most desperate but the most common attempt to win a husband's affection. Some women spend many lonely and anxious years struggling through repeated pregnancies, secretly hoping to obtain the love and devotion of their husband. Some will not go quite that far but will resort to buying tickets to a ballgame, going to movies, fancy meals, and vacations, even to the point of digging themselves deeply into debt. They try to secretly pacify the unsettling feeling within the marriage.

Rejection can cause you to think negatively about yourself. Jacob was not interested in Leah's love because he loved Rachel, and Leah was depressed because Jacob rejected her. Rejection is painful and causes us to think less of ourselves. Psychologists claim that 77 percent of what we think about ourselves is negative. Perhaps 100 percent of what Leah thought about herself was negative.

The secrets of the psychologists. Psychologists are always digging into our past and trying to help us put meaning into our chaotic world. They ask "feely, touchy" questions about our private life, like, "How do you feel about your mother?" and "How do you feel about your father?" They search for secrets and hidden events or messages that regulate our behavior. Simeon never experienced or witnessed his father loving his mother and throughout his boyhood only heard Jacob complain about the dirty trick Laban and Leah played on him. His mother was a puppet. She was ugly and depressing. She was a desperate housewife who would do anything for love. Imagine the psychological impact this must have had on Simeon. How would her secret life shape his future? What challenges did he face? What example did he have during his childhood? Certainly nothing he would wish to emulate.

3) The eavesdropping fetus. According to Genesis 29:33, Leah believed that God heard she was hated and rejected by Jacob. But strangely enough, the fetus (later to be named Simeon) also heard how his mother was hated. Simeon could feel and hear words of hatred and cruelty while he was still in his mother's womb. Simeon could hear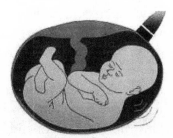

Figure 2.2

the agonizing sound of his mother as she asked, "Why don't you love me, Jacob?" It is a documented fact that a fetus can recognize sounds from the womb. In the summer of 1991, *Newsweek* published an article entitled, "Do You Hear What I Hear?" The article suggested that twenty weeks after conception, fetuses begin to respond to small stimulations. Even earlier during a pregnancy a fetus can respond to pain.

Could Simeon really experience his mother's pain? Did he understand suffering and rejection before he was born? Simeon, only a fetus, was eavesdropping. Simeon listened from the darkness of his mother's womb, and he could feel her painful emotions. He could feel bitterness, cruelty, injustice, and even resentment. For a period of nine months, each night the fetus heard the weeping voice of a rejected mother. How did the sounds of a lamenting, pregnant mother affect the personality of Simeon? From the womb, this unborn child heard the family secret. Simeon knew the family secret. The secret was that the father hated the mother. This would help explain Simeon's later anger and violent temper that drove him to murder in Genesis 32.

4) Instruments of cruelty. While lying on his deathbed, Jacob cursed Simeon and Levi's anger. Jacob said, "For in their anger they slew a man ... Cursed be their anger" (Genesis 49:6).

"Simeon and Levi are brethren; instruments of cruelty are in their habitations. O my soul, come not thou into their secret; unto their assembly, mine honour, be not thou united: for in their anger they slew a man, and in their selfwill they digged down a wall. Cursed be their anger, for it was fierce; and their wrath, for it was cruel: I will divide them in Jacob, and scatter them in Israel" (Genesis 49:5–7).

Jacob called Simeon and Levi "instruments of cruelty." He compared these sons to inanimate objects. He did not call them, "instruments of worship," "instruments of praise," or "instruments of righteousness" but of "cruelty." The secret of the two brothers was their cruelty. But let us focus on Simeon. His anger caused him to become an instrument of pain. His anger reflected the anger of his mother. Why was Simeon angry? He inherited a pain-filled world.

Simeon was the second son of Jacob and Leah and the father of the tribe of Simeon, one of the twelve tribes of Israel. The Hebrew meaning of his name is, "God has heard that I was unloved" (Genesis 29:33). Simeon symbolizes people who intentionally and secretly hear private conversations. He is a man full of anger. Anger is one letter short of "danger." Simeon was an angry and dangerous man. He was angry because he felt he had no control over his life.

Reasons to be angry. As a young boy, Simeon heard many things that affected his life: 1) From his mother's womb he heard his mother's painful cries of rejection; 2) he heard news that his sister had been kidnapped and raped; 3) he heard that the man who raped his sister wanted to marry her; 4) he heard that the rapist and his family wanted to be adopted into the family of Jacob and inherit the family's wealth.

Joseph chose to keep Simeon as a prisoner to guarantee his brothers would return with Benjamin. Louis Ginzberg tells us in his book, *"Legends of the Bible,"* that Simeon was the one who insisted they kill Joseph. Simeon was the one who threw him into the pit. He was full of secret passion and revenge. Privately he was fierce and uncontrollable. His sword, which should only have been a weapon of defense, became an instrument of aggressive violence.

Simeon's sister raped in a secret place. After Jacob led his eleven sons back to Canaan (following twenty years in Haran), Dinah was searching for new girlfriends in her new neighborhood. While walking through her new town and being social, a young man named Shechem from the leading family of a nearby town saw her, brought her to a quiet, secret place, and raped her. Rapes are almost always committed in secret places. How many dirty, rape secrets have marred and twisted innocent personalities? Shechem raped Dinah and then took her back to his home. Even though Dinah was a victim of rape, Shechem fell in love with her. Shechem, the rapist, asked his father to "get me this young woman as a wife" (Genesis 34:4). Shechem's father approached Jacob with the intent of negotiating a marriage contract. Simeon heard of this marriage proposal and was furious.

Gossip in the field or "I heard it through the grapevine." Simeon heard of the marriage proposal while working in the field. He overheard men talking about how his sister, Dinah, had been raped by Shechem (Genesis 34:7). Bad news travels fast. Dinah was the only daughter of Jacob and Leah. Dinah's name is mentioned in Genesis 30:21 but never mentioned again in scriptures until Genesis 34.

A little bird told Simeon. How did Simeon hear of the marriage proposal so quickly? Was it possible that an eavesdropper was able to get wind of it? It is amazing how people find things out. Bad news travels fast. There are eavesdroppers everywhere. I have asked myself why people whisper. Do they whisper to avoid disturbing others, or do they whisper to avoid an undetected eavesdropper? Sometimes it is necessary to whisper because some people are dying to know your private business. The Bible warns us to govern our thoughts and words because of eavesdroppers. The little bird that eavesdrops reminds us of the words of King Solomon. "Curse not the king, no not in thy thought; and curse not the rich in thy bedchamber: for a bird of the air shall carry the voice, and that which hath wings shall tell the matter" (Ecclesiastes 10:20).

Figure 2.3

Walls have ears! The Bible says be careful what you say because even a bird could overhear your conversation and report your words (Ecclesiastes 10:20). Maybe this is where the word, "stool pigeon," comes from. Nevertheless, Simeon learned of Shechem's crime and sought to destroy him and his entire family.

5) Be angry, but do not sin. "Be ye angry, and sin not: let not the sun go down upon your wrath" (Ephesians 4:26). Jacob's sons were very angry and committed a horrendous sin.

Even though Jacob's only daughter had been raped, he befriended the Shechemites. However, his sons remained furious by Shechem's heinous act. The Shechemites believed that Jacob and his sons were God fearing, peaceable, and harmless men. They said,

"These men are peaceable with us; therefore let them dwell in the land, and trade therein; for the land, behold, it is large enough for them; let us take their daughters to us for wives, and let us give them our daughters. Only herein will the men consent unto us for to dwell with us, to be one people, if every male among us be circumcised as they are circumcised. Shall not their cattle and their substance and every beast of theirs be ours? Only let us consent unto them, and they will dwell with us" (Genesis 34:21-23).

The above verses tell us that the Shechemites discussed several benefits of intermarriage with Jacob's family. Someone was eavesdropping while the Shechemites counted the benefits they would gain by marrying into Jacob's family. The marriage proposal consisted of many benefits to the Shechemite family, such as:

- Jacob dropping the rape charges and living peaceably with the Shechemite family.

- The Shechemites allowing Jacob and his family to dwell in the land.

- The Shechemite family becoming circumcised and following Jehovah.

- Shechem marrying Dinah.

- The Shechemite family acquiring increased business trading opportunities.

- Continued opportunity for intermarrying, therefore creating further unity between the two families.

- The Shechemites inheriting a portion of Jacob's livestock and property.

The Shechemites were an honorable family, for the most part, but the sons of Jacob were hot-headed, unyielding, and unscrupulous. Simeon pretended to be in agreement with the benefits laid out, and under the guise of requiring religious observance made the

Shechemites agree to be circumcised. All the men of the Shechemite tribe submitted to the rite (Genesis 34:25–29).

When Shechem and his father (Hamor) requested marriage, Dinah's brothers and father conducted the negotiations. The sons were secretly furious that a man who had raped their sister was now going to marry her. This was ridiculous, they thought. They hid their anger, and Jacob promised to permit the marriage if the men of the city would accept circumcision. The men of the city agreed to circumcision, which consists of a surgical removal of the outer skin from the penis. This surgery is excruciatingly painful for any man, and the Shechemites were unable to walk after their incisions. While they were incapacitated by this operation, two of Dinah's brothers, Simeon and Levi, entered the city, killed all the men, and brought their sister home. Simeon and Levi took advantage of the wholesale circumcision by attacking the Shechemites on the third day, when they knew that the recuperating men would be unable to defend themselves. Simeon was the leader of this attack, and it was a shameful, vile, and senseless deed that displayed utter insensibility of immoral behavior.

Justification for murder. Simeon and Levi felt justified in committing murder, but Jacob later complained that his sons had put him in an awkward position. Simeon and Levi responded by asking their father, "Should he deal with our sister as with an harlot?" (Genesis 34:31). Simeon and Levi's secret agenda was devilish. The brothers tricked the Shechemites and massacred all the males because one of them had raped their sister Dinah. Was this secret agenda right? Do you have a secret agenda? Their secret agenda's deed was an act of grave immorality and an outrage against decency and family honor.

"And Jacob said to Simeon and Levi, Ye have troubled me to make me to stink among the inhabitants of the land, among the Canaanites and the Perizzites: and I being few in number, they shall gather themselves together against me, and slay me; and I shall be destroyed, I and my house" (Genesis 34:30).

Jacob scold his sons for slaughtering the Shechemites. "Open rebuke is better than secret love" (Proverbs 27:5). But nearly twenty-five years later, Jacob recalled this incident. He charged his other sons not to fellowship with Simeon and Levi. He said, "...come not thou into their secret...." (Genesis 49:6). He warned his ten sons to separate from their counsel and separate from their thinking and conversation. Jacob charged them not to associate with these two murderers. Do not unite with them! (Genesis 49:6).

Simeon's secret fault. We all have secret faults. God knows of these flaws in our character and understands these secret errors, and we must ask for healing and cleansing. Did Leah have to feel the self-rejection and self-hatred because of Jacob? Could she have chosen to be cleansed of this secret error in her perception of self-worth? It was not her fault that Jacob was tricked, just as it was not her fault that Jacob simply did not love her. Her self-pity led to secret pain that only God could heal. "Who can understand his errors? Cleanse thou me from secret faults" (Psalm 19:12).

The eavesdropper never has good news. Simeon's life was so full of bad news that it caused him to become a very angry man. He could not control his anger, and angry men are dangerous. Proverbs 22:25 admonished us to stay away from angry men. "Make no friendship with an angry man; and with a furious man thou shalt not go: Lest thou learn his ways, and get a snare to thy soul" (Proverb 22:25).

The mismanagement of anger. Jacob rebuked Simeon and Levi for killing the Shechemite family, as he was quite angry with them for their reckless murders. Jacob cursed their anger and not Simeon and Levi themselves. Notice how Jacob called down a curse on his sons' anger.

Nations, communities and churches are weakened when it produces people who cannot control their anger or fail to be angered at all. Someone said, "If you do not stand for something, you will fall for anything." When you see an injustice it should anger you and cause righteous indignation. Righteous indignation is typically a reactive emotion to be angered over perceived mistreatment, insult, or malice. People who cannot get angry are people who do not understand anything about justice and boundaries. Simeon became lethargic and apathetic because Jacob cursed his anger. He would lose his ability to get angry. People who cannot get angry are people who are always victimized. It seemed as if Jacob damned their anger to frigidity. After the curse, Simeon lacked righteous indignation. He never got angry. He allowed men to abuse him and walk over him, and never stood against anything. Paul wrote to the church at Ephesus to instruct them about anger. He said anger is not a bad thing, just do not sin when you get angry. Ephesians 4:26 said, "Be ye angry, and sin not: let not the sun go down upon your wrath:".

John Henry Cardinal Newman stated, "Inanimate things cannot stir our affection ....[3]" Simeon's sense of right and wrong became inanimate, and his inability to get angry was a sign that he was afraid of the separateness that comes with telling his secret truths. Because Simeon's anger was cursed, the tribe of Simeon would never produce any "heroes, great men or women, leaders, or prophets." The tribe lacked passion and feelings of excitement. We shall see in chapter three, to follow, that the curse against Levi was reversed and God blessed him. However, there is no record that Simeon ever repented. Simeon was the third-largest tribe in Israel in the first census (Numbers 1:23, 2:13), but by the second census they had plummeted to be the smallest tribe of all! Jacob's curse against Simeon was prophetic because his tribe was reduced by 62 percent. The tribe of Simeon numbered 59,300 fighting men at the first census in the wilderness (Numbers 1:23, 2:13). However, the second census, taken after the journey through the wilderness, the tribe of Simeon numbered only 22,200 (Numbers 26:12–14), a reduction of 37,100 fighting men. There is no record that God ever used this tribe in any great way because of the mismanagement of their anger.

---

[3]   Martin, Brian, *John Henry Newman: His Life & Work*, Continuum International Publishing Group, January 2001.

Anger can seriously cloud our ability to live. Did Simeon have a secret anger management problem? We can assume that Simeon knew a lot of confidential information – good and evil. This information may have caused him to feel sad. King Solomon said, "in much wisdom there is much sorrow" (Ecclesiastes 1:18). Sometimes knowing a lot of negative information can make you sad or angry. God knew the pain Simeon felt. Many people put on a happy face in public, making everyone believe they are content while secretly they are very depressed and anguished. Simeon was forced to witness rejection, deception, and secret love his entire life. Being a child living through this pain may have caused a depression-like emotion that God surely able to mend. Perhaps you, a friend, or a loved one has felt or is feeling secret depression. The secret consumes you and festers the longer you hold on to it. Pause for a moment and ask God to bring you out of your secret depression, heal the wounds of the past, and guide you into a happier future. "Shall not God search this out? For he knoweth the secrets of the heart" (Psalm 44:21).

The descendants of Simeon scattered. A comparison of the cities assigned to Simeon with those assigned to Judah (Joshua 15:20–63, 19:1–9; 1 Chronicles 4:28–33) makes it appear that the tribe of Simeon had been assimilated into the tribe of Judah, thus fulfilling Jacob's prophecy (Genesis 49:5–7).

"I will divide them in Jacob." These were the prophetic words of Jacob. Simeon would be divided from his brothers, and the tribe of Simeon was divided and scattered. Simeon did not really understand the ramifications of his father's prophecy.

6) Warning signs of covert eavesdropping or bugging. The spirit of Simeon (eavesdropping) is alive and well in the twenty-first century. If any of the following warning signs apply to you, there is a good chance eavesdropping or wiretapping is in progress.

- Others know your confidential business or professional trade secrets.

- Secret meetings and bids seem to be less than secret.

- People seem to know your activities when they should not.

- You have noticed strange sounds or volume changes on your cell or phone lines.

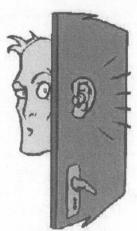

Figure 2.4

- You have noticed static, popping, or scratching on your cell or phone line.

- Your phone often rings and nobody is there, or you hear a very faint tone or high-pitched squeal/beep.

- You can hear a tone on your line when your phone is on the hook.

- Your AM/FM radio has suddenly developed strange interference.

- Your car radio suddenly starts "getting weird."

- Your television has suddenly developed strange interference.

- You have been the victim of a break-in but nothing was taken.

- Electrical wall plates appear to have been moved slightly or "jarred."

- A dime-sized discoloration has suddenly appeared on the wall or ceiling.

- One of your vendors just gave you an electronic device such as a desk radio, alarm clock, lamp, small TV, boom box, or CD player.

- A small bump or deformation has appeared on the vinyl baseboard near the floor.

- A smoke detector, clock, lamp, or exit sign in your office or home looks slightly crooked, has a small hole in its surface, or has a quasi-reflective surface.

- Certain types of items have "just appeared" in your office or home and nobody seems to know how they got there.

- Telephone, cable, plumbing, or air conditioning repair people show up to do work when they were not called.

- Furniture has been moved slightly and no one knows why.

- An eavesdropper sends you a copy of your private conversations.

POINTS TO PONDER

The Secret of Simeon—Eavesdropping. Simeon was Jacob's second son. His name means, "hearing". His mother was also Leah. Simeon heard secret information that drove him to commit murder. He is symbolic of people who intentionally eavesdrop, and this chapter provides many examples of Biblical characters that practiced eavesdropping. Simeon's grandmother, Rebekah, was eavesdropping when she heard Isaac preparing to bless Esau in his tent. Years later,

Simeon was in the field and heard the news that his sister Dinah had been raped. Like his grandmother, he was eavesdropping.

- Eavesdropping is an intentional act of secretly listening to confidential conversations.

- You must be careful what you say because you do not know who can be trusted. There could very well be a spy, gossipper, or a "wannabe" "in the know" eavesdropper lurking in the darkness.

- More and more businesses are using sophisticated electronic equipment and devices to record confidential discussions.

- Eavesdroppers frequently mislead and misquote people and disseminate incorrect information.

- People who eavesdrop seek to hear confidential information for the purpose of gossip and personal gain.

- There are many examples of eavesdroppers in the Bible.

- Psychologists claim that 77 percent of what we think about ourselves is negative.

- It is a documented fact that a fetus can recognize sounds from within the womb.

- The Bible says to be careful what you say because even a "bird" could overhear your conversation and report your words (Ecclesiastes 10:20).

- No man has ever overheard a private conversation between God and man.

- "Open rebuke is better than secret love" (Proverbs 27:5).

- Who can understand his errors? Cleanse thou me from secret faults (Psalm 19:12).

Simeon heard many secrets. 1 Corinthians 15:33 says, "Be not deceived: evil communications corrupt good manners."Did Simeon corrupt Levi's behavior? Simeon was a murderer but he had an accomplice, Levi. Let us look closer at Levi's secret issues.

CHAPTER 3

Jacob's Fear

Jacob

Canaanites

Perizzites

THE SECRET OF LEVI

SECRET RELATIONSHIPS

"Simeon and Levi are brethren; instruments of cruelty are in their habitations. O my soul, come not thou into their secret; unto their assembly, mine honor, be not thou united: for in their anger they slew a man, and in their selfwill they digged down a wall. Cursed be their anger, for it was fierce; and their wrath, for it was cruel: I will divide them in Jacob, and scatter them in Israel" (Genesis 49:5–7).

Secret relationships can best be illustrated by the story of Harvey and Connie. While Harvey takes a hot shower, his cell phone rings but he is unaware of it. His wife, Connie, picks up the phone and politely says, "Hello." But there is no response. Connie hears the soft breaths of the caller. Without a spoken word, she senses that the caller is a female and feels that the unknown caller is intentionally hiding her identity. Connie inquires again, "Hello. Is anybody there?" There is silence for about three more seconds. Then the unknown caller abruptly hangs up. Connie closes her husband's cell phone. She wonders who it was and why a person would refuse to identify him or herself. She questions … just for a moment … whether Harvey is having an affair or, more troubling, if he is on the down-low.

Yes, Harvey is guilty of infidelity, and secret relationships are everywhere. Estimates of infidelity in the United States range from 20% to 50%.[4] One estimate rated the percentage of all Americans who would have an extramarital affair during their lives as high as 70%.[5] Secret relationships are not limited to infidelity. We see secret relationships among politicians, religious people, rich and poor, and black and white. Some people call this process networking. Networking is the process of developing relationships with people who can either directly or indirectly assist you with your career planning process or any other profitable endeavor. Networking is often overlooked but it is an invaluable tool that can help you do many things. Networking is also a powerful way to communicate and get things done. However, secret networking is even more powerful because you do not know who is connected with whom, where someone's loyalty starts or ends, and who is talking in secret. You should be careful about making friends too quickly because you do not know who knows whom. You do not know all the connections!

The first secret relationship. In the Garden of Eden, Eve and the serpent had a seemingly secret (talking) relationship (Genesis 3). There is no biblical evidence that suggests Adam was aware of Eve's conversations with the serpent. It appeared that the serpent was no stranger to Eve, as they talked as if they were familiar with each other. The serpent told Eve that there were no negative consequences to disobeying God's Word. In fact, the serpent said her relationship

---

4   Lampe, P. E. (ed.) *Adultery in the United States: Close Encounters of the Sixth (or Seventh) Kind.* Buffalo: Prometheus Books, 1987.
5   *Marriage and Divorce Today,* June 1, 1987, cited in Fisher, Helen E. *Anatomy of Love: the natural history of monogamy, adultery and divorce.* New York: W. W. Norton & Company, Inc., 1992, p. 86.

with God would change if she ate of the forbidden tree. The serpent said that she would be "like God". Eve followed the serpent's bad counsel and, as a result, was evicted from the Garden of Eden and condemned to death.

Secret relationships in the Bible. The Bible is full of secret relationships. Below are a few examples:

- **A secret relationship in the family**. During a famine, Joseph chose to maintain a secret relationship with his brothers when they visited Egypt. Joseph covered his face and spoke roughly to his brothers through an interpreter in order to disguise his identity (Genesis 42:7).

- **Two men's secret relationship**. David and Jonathan established a secret relationship because of the jealousy and hatred of King Saul towards David. David and Jonathan's love was deeper than that of a man and woman (2 Samuel 1:26).

- **Secret relationships exposed**. King Hosea established a secret relationship with King So of Egypt. The king of Assyria found out about this secret alliance, felt it was a conspiracy against him, and then bound King Hosea and threw him in prison where he died (2 Kings 17:4).

- **A queen who is incognito?** Queen Esther and her uncle Mordecai concealed her Jewish heritage from King Ahasuerus. Being born in Shushan and her parents being dead, Esther managed to convince everyone she was of Persian descent (Esther 2:1–20).

- **A secret meeting with the Rabbi**. A Pharisee named Nicodemus (a ruler of the Jews) met with Jesus at night in order to initiate a secret relationship with him (John 3:1).

- **Sleeping with the enemies**. Judas Iscariot lodged many nights with Christ and his disciples but maintained a secret relationship among the chief priests and Pharisees in order to betray Jesus (John 18:3).

Mysteries of the Godhead. The relationship between the Father, Son, and Holy Ghost is a great mystery. God is so great that he is beyond human comprehension. He is so great that we cannot hold him to a numerical system. Oneness believers and Trinitarians continue to debate the godhead issue. Is God three persons or three manifestations of one God? Modalistic Monarchianism, also known as Modalism, is the view that God variously manifested Himself as the Father (primarily in the Old Testament), other times as the Son (primarily from Jesus' conception to His ascension), and other times as the Holy Spirit (primarily after Jesus' ascension into Heaven). Modalistic Monarchianism or Modalism teaches that God has simply revealed Himself in three different modes, and that He is not three Persons. The revelation of the godhead is a great mystery and incomprehensible to mortal man without revelation of the Holy Spirit (1 Timothy 3:16). However, the Bible teaches its students to "prove all things; hold fast that which is good" (1 Thessalonians 5:21).

In the scriptures, mysteries are unknown areas that are eventually revealed to the reader.

Below are a few scriptures that assure us that God's mysteries are now revealed:

- "Unto you it is given to know the mystery of the Kingdom of God ..." (Mark 4:11).

- "Behold I show you a mystery; we shall not all sleep, but we shall be changed" (1 Corinthians 15:51).

- "Having made known unto us the mystery ..." (Ephesians 1:9).

- "Even the mystery which has been hid from ages and from generations, but now is made manifest ..." (Colossians 1:26).

This chapter is about the power of secret relationships. As we shall see, Levi symbolizes concealed relationships. As a young boy he was adversely affected by how his mother was treated. Like his brother Simeon, Levi saw his mother weep for lack of love and affection. He saw his father struggle between his anger and his duty to love her.

In order to understand the secrets of Levi, you must understand the power of secret relationships. As we analyze the secret relationships of Levi, we will consider the following factors:

1) Secrets of a honeymoon
2) The secret relationship between two brothers
3) Secret relationships and alliances
4) Secret anger and public cruelty
5) Secret of reversing the curse
6) Hiding in the tabernacle

1) Secrets of a honeymoon. In return for seven years of labor, Laban (Jacob's uncle) promised to give his daughter, Rachel, to Jacob as his wife. However, on the honeymoon night, Laban secretly substituted Rachel for her sister Leah. He did this by concealing Leah's face with a veil. Jacob was probably drunk during the wedding festivities, and he was furious when he awoke the next day and discovered that the woman he had slept with was not the woman he loved. Laban's marriage proposal was just a scam to keep Jacob working for another seven years! The marriage between Jacob and Leah got off on a bad foot and stayed that way, doomed by Laban's deceitful plan (Genesis 29:26).

Laban obviously put Leah in an awkward position. A drunken Jacob, in a dark tent, consummated the marriage. Jacob whispered sweet nothings into Leah's ear all night, saying, "Rachel, my love ... Rachel, my darling ... I waited seven years for you." In the darkness of the tent, Leah experienced true passion and love. It was the first and last time that Leah would ever receive Jacob's love and passion.

An inability to communicate. When Jacob awoke he was horrified. He discovered Leah underneath his arm even though he had been led by Laban to believe he had married Rachel. He married the plain, unattractive, eldest daughter (Genesis 29:17). The voice of Leah is only heard when she named her children. Leah was quiet and unassuming woman. Nevertheless, Jacob thought hard and long about the dirty trick Laban and Leah played on him. I can hear Jacob asking himself, "Why didn't Leah communicate? Why didn't she speak up? Why didn't she say something when I was making love to her? Why didn't she say, 'Hey, Jacob, my name is Leah'?" Jacob believed that Leah was a collaborator in her father's conspiracy, and he would never trust her. The cake he ate at the wedding would be the cake that gave him indigestion for the rest of his life.

A secret lonely heart. Leah tasted Jacob's love only once, and that occurred when Jacob mistakenly thought Leah was Rachel on their honeymoon night. Leah was hungry for his secret love. "Love ceases to be pleasure, when it ceases to be a secret," says Aphra Behn[6]. For Leah, even Jacob's secret love was absent. The loneliest place in the world is a human heart absent of love. Leah's marriage was like arthritis—she had to learn to live with it. Even though Leah gave birth to six sons, Jacob still did not trust or love her. The foundation of a marriage is trust. Leah knew that her babies could hold the marriage together, but they could not win Jacob's love. What a sad story we find here—a woman who thought the birth of children would cause her husband to fall in love with her ... but Jacob never did.

The secrets of Levi's mother. Leah desperately wanted to connect with her husband. She was a lonely woman. Leah lacked personal

---

[6] Behn, Aphra. *The Works of Aphra Behn, III: The Fair Jilt and Other Stories*. Janet Todd, ed. Columbus, OH: Ohio State UP, 1995 (*Aphra Behn, 1640-1689, was the first professional woman writer in English literature*).

attractiveness, and she was weary, plain, and dull. Jacob failed to see anything beautiful about her. Leah's name means weary. This is a horrible name for a young lady, especially in Old Testament times when names were chosen to capture the essence of a person's character.

Leah lived with a man who did not love her. They had little in common and Leah asked over and over, "What can I do to get this man to love me?"

Affection from Jacob was all that Leah longed for. Even a secret relationship would be acceptable to Leah. Leah wanted to be loved in the dark, for that is how their union started—in a dark tent (Genesis 29:25). In fact, some people enjoy relationships in the dark. They enjoy late, secret cell phone calls, secret gifts, secret affections, and secret affairs. Leah was desperate to be loved and was willing to do anything to make the relationship work.

Leah prayed for a third child (see Figure 3.1). Even though she had already given birth to two sons and still received none of Jacob's love, Leah believed that a third child would get her what she desired. For the third time she failed to understand that having sex and having babies were not equal to intimacy and a healthy relationship. Yet, Leah dreamed of being one with Jacob. Like any wife, she wanted to connect with her husband. She wanted to share his dreams, his pains, his triumphs, and his failures in life. Leah so deeply desired a relationship that she named her third son "Levi," which means, "joining."

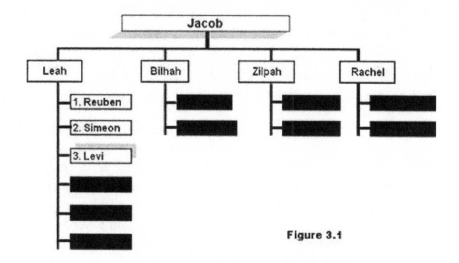

Figure 3.1

Webster's Dictionary defines "joining" as, "to place together, bring together, connect, fasten; combine; to make into one unit." "And she conceived again, and bare a son; and said, Now, this time will my husband be joined unto me, because I have born him three sons: therefore was his name called Levi" (Genesis 29:34).

Even after a third son, Jacob remained cold and indifferent toward Leah, but Jacob seemed "too good" for Leah to leave him. If she left Jacob, what man would replace him? He was the son of the wealthy Isaac and the grandson of a powerful man named Abraham. He was handsome and rich, and Leah knew he was a good catch for any girl in Canaan.

Too good to leave, too bad stay. Jacob was too good to leave but too bad to stay. He did not love Leah. He was a trickster, a liar, and a polygamist. A polygamist is a person who has two or more wives at the same time. In the Old Testament era and culture, polygamy was an acceptable practice but not God's perfect will for marriage. Throughout his story, Jacob failed to show any affection towards Leah. Jacob slept with her, but his motivation was lust, not love.

Jacob was angry with Laban for his trickery, he was angry that Leah could have children while Rachel could not, and he was angry because Rachel never said anything good about God. She was just a good-looking sister without a praise in her heart! He was also angry because he was such a failure in life, and angry men are dangerous. Leah could not pacify Jacob's anger, not even with giving him healthy sons.

Looking for a relationship in the wrong places. And for Jacob it was just that—sex! But Leah wanted more than sex. She wanted a relationship. She wanted to be joined or connected with Jacob. She believed a secret gift could ignite his passion, and her secret gift is Levi. Leah gives her body to Jacob in secret to pacify his anger and to give hope to her dream. His midnight kisses and touches lacked passion and intimacy. Women can feel a man's unspoken anger, and Jacob's anger blocked Leah from making a heart connection. However, Leah had a burning, secret desire of winning his love, so she accepted his cold, passionless kisses. He was a bad lover, but she remembered the honeymoon night and the hot passion he had expressed. The passion was too good to leave, but he was saving that passion for her sister, Rachel. Leah knew that something was wrong in the relationship. She wanted his love at any cost, but Jacob never granted that wish.

2) The secret relationship between two brothers. "Simeon and Levi are brethren; instruments of cruelty are in their habitations. O my soul, come not thou into their secret; unto their assembly, mine honour, be not thou united: for in their anger they slew a man, and in their selfwill they digged down a wall. Cursed be their anger, for it was fierce; and their wrath, for it was cruel: I will divide them in Jacob, and scatter them in Israel" (Genesis 49:5–7).

The above speech, usually referred to as Jacob's blessings to his sons, is definitely not a blessing as it concerns the first three sons of Jacob. Reuben, Simeon, and Levi are linked together by condemnation, guilt, sin, shame, and retribution. But Simeon and Levi are brothers who possessed the same disposition. Genesis 49:5 states that, "Simeon and Levi are brethren." This phrase implies that they have the same attitude and same mind. There are twelve sons, but these are the only two brothers whose prophecies were linked together. Jacob stated that Levi and Simeon were brothers whose tempers ruled their lives.

3) Secret relationships and alliances. "And Jacob said to Simeon and Levi, Ye have troubled me to make me to stink among the inhabitants of the land, among the Canaanites and the Perizzites: and I being few in number, they shall gather themselves together against me, and slay me; and I shall be destroyed, I and my house" (Genesis 34:30).

Jacob told Levi and Simeon that they had caused him trouble. As described in chapter two, Levi and Simeon had killed the entire male side of the Shechemite family. Jacob stated that his sons had made him "stink" among the people of his new community. How could he share his testimony of Jehovah's power and love after his sons had committed such a horrendous crime? Jacob felt as if he had lost his testimony, and he further feared that his neighbors would retaliate against his family for the Shechemite massacre.

the Canaanites

the Perizzites

the Shechemites

Figure 3.2

Secret relationships cannot be altered. The above figure 3.2 shows the possible relationships between the Canaanites, the Perizzites, and the Shechemites. Did the Shechemites have secret relationship with the Canaanites and Perizzites? This was Jacob's greatest fear. Jacob feared that his family would be destroyed by the Canaanites and Perizzites for slaughtering the Shechemites. There was no public relationship or alliance between the Canaanites and Perizzites as far as Jacob could tell, but he was concerned with the secret relationships and alliances between his enemies and neighbors. Jacob understood the difference between the power of public and secret alliances. Conventional wisdom says that secret alliances are more conducive to war than public alliances because secret alliances cannot be deterred. Jacob was concerned that the Canaanites, Perizzites and Shechemites had a secret alliance and would soon attack his family. He felt helpless because of the possibility of secret relationships.

Jacob did not know if the Canaanites and Perizzites were going to attack, so his situation was tense. Robert Kann suggested that, "The desire to decrease tension is also incompatible with the concept of the secret alliance."[7] The pressure was so overwhelming that God directed Jacob to relocate his family and return to Bethel.

4) Secret anger and public cruelty. "Cursed be their anger, for it was fierce; and their wrath, for it was cruel" (Genesis 34:7).

Levi had been affected by the secret anger of his parents. Anger is what is known as a "secondary emotion," which means it comes after another feeling—usually pain, fear, or powerlessness. Secret emotions within the family caused bitterness, resentment, and anger in the heart and life of Levi. Each lie, deception, and withholding of vital choices can cause a large, secret stone to dam up brotherhood. Anger grows each day and affects each person within a family unit. Jacob knew the reason for murder. He gives a rationale for stupidity. He cried, "For in their anger they slew a man" (Genesis 49:6). Simeon

---

[7]   Robert Kann, "*Alliances Versus Ententes,*" *World Politics, Vol. 28, No. 4. (July 1976), pp. 614.*

and Levi's anger was fierce and led them to execute an entire family in madness. Even though Jacob confessed his love for Jehovah, his sons were a contradiction to his testimony. They committed an ugly and embarrassing act. On Jacob's deathbed, his disappointment was expressed in a curse against his two sons.

Who sought to kill Joseph? The Scriptures refer to Simeon and Levi when we see the word "brothers." Even though there are twelve sons, Simeon and Levi are the closest, and they appear to have a secret relationship. It was their intention to kill Joseph. "And they said one to his brother ... Come now therefore and let us slay him" (Genesis 37:19–20). Who are the "brothers" that were determined to kill Joseph?

Reuben planned to rescue Joseph at a later time, so it was not his intention to murder Joseph. Judah suggested that Joseph be sold into slavery, so murder was not in his heart. Dan and Gad, sons of Bilhah, and Naphtali and Asher, sons of Zilpah, were too young to plan a murder (Genesis 37:2). Issachar and Zebulun did not speak in front of their older brothers. Only Simeon and Levi remain, and their father called them, "brothers of cruelty." I believe it was Simeon and Levi who suggested that Joseph be murdered.

Levi's secret anger against animals. "And in their selfwill they digged down a wall" (Genesis 49:6). "Dig down a wall" refers to horses or cows whose tendons had been severed. When Simeon and Levi destroyed the Shechemites, they also destroyed the Shechemites' animals. Simeon and Levi took the cattle and horses and cut or detached their tendons. To hamstring an animal is to cut the tendon in its leg so that it is unable to walk. This is the severest type of animal abuse. Tendons can be found on an animal's hind legs. In Figure 3.3, the tendons from an animal's hind leg are noted by the circle. When Simeon and Levi cut the tendons, the animals were rendered useless and died with great suffering because they could not move.

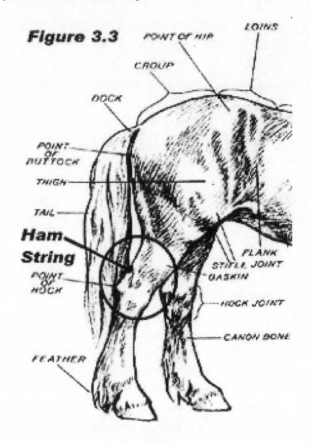

Figure 3.3

The awful scene demonstrated the extent of Levi and Simeon's anger. The key problem was their lack of self-control. "He that is soon angry dealeth foolishly: and a man of wicked devices is hated" (Proverbs 14:17).

There were many circumstances and characters in the Bible who practiced displaced anger. Here is a list of a just few:

- Abel's secret relationship with God made Cain angry. It was anger that caused Cain to slay Abel (Genesis 4:4).

- Regarding Joseph, the Bible says, "And when his brethren saw that their father loved him more than all the brothers, they hated him and could not speak peaceably to him" (Genesis 37:4), which means the brothers all hated Joseph even though they pretended to love him in their father's presence.

- They angered Moses and caused him to speak irrationally (Psalm 106: 32–33).

- Balaam's donkey angered him (Numbers. 22: 21–31).

- The Bible relates that when the sons of Jacob heard of Dinah's rape, "The men were grieved, and they were very angry" (Genesis 34:7).

- Saul's anger stirred up insecurity and jealousy towards David (1 Samuel 18:8).

- Naaman the Leper was angry because he was told to take a wash in the Jordan River (2 Kings 5:9–12).

- Nebuchadnezzar was angry because three Hebrew boys refused to worship his god (Daniel 3: 19).

- Herod was angry with the wise men and killed the children of Bethlehem (Matthew 2:16).

- In the story of the prodigal son, the oldest brother was angry and envious of his younger brother because his father had blessed him (Luke 15: 25–30).

5) Secrets of reversing the curse. "For in their anger they slew a man ... Cursed be their anger ..." (Genesis 34:5–7). Note that Jacob cursed their anger ... not them. According to *Nelson's Illustrated Bible Dictionary*, a curse is a prayer for injury, harm, or misfortune to befall someone. A curse is defined as, "the invocation of supernatural power to inflict harm upon someone or something." In biblical times, a curse was considered to be more than a mere wish that evil would befall someone—it was believed to possess the power to bring about the evil the curser spoke. We ought to learn, in the expression of our zeal for a spiritual life, to distinguish between the sinner and the sin. Remember, God hates your sin, but while you were yet sinners Christ died for you.

"I will divide them in Jacob, and scatter them in Israel" (Genesis 49:5–7). Like the Tower of Babel, the construction project in Genesis 16, Jacob desired that his sons would experience the misfortune of being divided and scattered. "I will divide them in Jacob" refers to Simeon, and "I will scatter them in Israel" refers to Levi.

Jacob's curse against Simeon was prophetic (his tribe was decimated), but there was a great difference between the curses. It is interesting that Jacob uses the names Jacob and Israel in his prophetic curse. Jacob was a dishonorable name that meant supplanter, heel-catcher, and sinner. It refers to the old nature. Israel, on the other hand, means "a prince with God." Why are both names mentioned? One suggestion is a foreshadowing of the histories of Simeon and Levi. I will divide in Jacob refers to Simeon and I will scatter them in Israel refers to Levi.

Jacob's curse against Levi was prophetic. When Levi became the custodian of the Law of Moses and religion, Levi's curse was removed.

Levi was used in service of the Lord. The Levitical tribe maintained a special relationship with God because they were chosen by God to care for holy things, manage the tabernacle, and assist in sacrifices (Numbers 3:5, 8:14). The three essentials of the Levitical priesthood were:

1. Commissioned by God.

2. Separated to God.

3. Allowed to a special relationship with God by coming near to him (Exodus 28; Numbers 16:5).

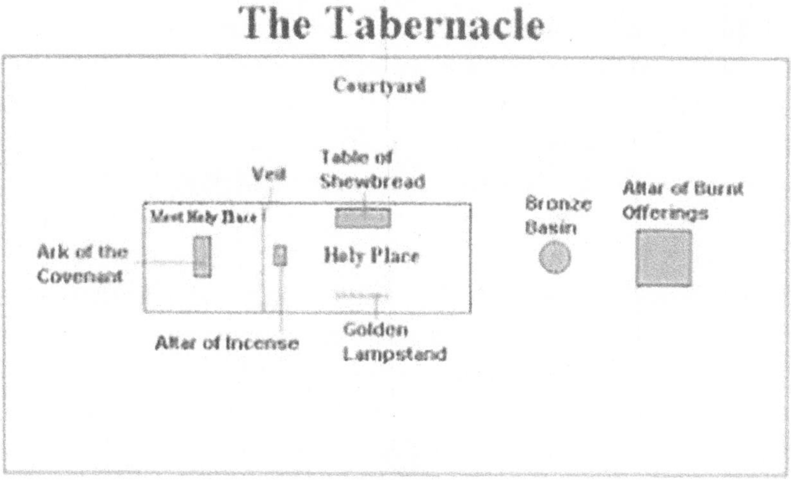

The Tabernacle

Figure 3.4

Horizontal and vertical ministry. At the time of the removal of Levi's curse, the Lord separated the tribe of Levi to bear the ark of the covenant of the Lord, to stand before the Lord to minister unto him, and to bless his name, unto this day (Deuteronomy 10:8). God chose the entire tribe of Levi to be his ministers and desired a special relationship with them. As God moved through the camp of Israel, he selected the tribe of Levi to become his ministers not only to minister for him to the people (horizontal), but also to minister directly to him (vertical). Because of Levi's separation from his brothers, we read in the next verse that, "therefore Levi hath no part nor inheritance with his brethren, the LORD is his inheritance, according as thy God hath promised him" (Deuteronomy 10:9).

Secret relationship means secret inheritance. When Israel finally arrived in the Promised Land, Joshua divided out to each tribe a portion of land. However, the tribe of Levi was not given a natural possession, for in the Lord alone he was to find his inheritance. Levi was to minister to the Lord. The Lord, in turn, would make sure all his needs were met.

How Levi's curse was removed—the secret relationship. In Exodus 32, Moses delayed his coming and the people grew restless.

They did not know what happened to Moses, so they made a golden calf and began to worship it. When Moses returned, he was astounded and saddened. The Bible says, "Then Moses stood in the gate of the camp, and said, Who is on the LORD's side? Let him come unto me. And all the sons of Levi gathered themselves together unto him" (Exodus 32:26). Levi joined Moses, and the tribe of Levi then goes against its fellow Jews in a violent attempt to destroy the golden calf, its instigators, and its ideas and beliefs. From that day forward the curse would be removed. Levi's curse was removed but Simeon's curse remained. When a person accepts Christ it removes all curses. Moses was a type of Christ and when Levi accepted Moses' invitation to join him, the curse of Jacob was removed. Paul reminded us that our curse has also been removed, "Christ hath redeemed us from the curse of the law, being made a curse for us: for it is written, Cursed is every one that hangeth on a tree" (Galatians 3:13).

Since the day Levi joined Moses, the curse was removed from his family. The Levites became the holy consecrated tribe. They were to teach, and they were in charge of the religious services. They were no longer instruments of cruelty because God changed them. Levi was given a new nature because "he stood on the Lord's side".

6) Hiding in the tabernacle. The tribe of Levi was responsible for leading all the other tribes of Israel in worship to God. Only members of the tribe of Levi knew how to handle the components of this portable tabernacle; their responsibilities and objectives were:

- To preserve and transmit the law (Leviticus 10:11; Deuteronomy 17:18, 33:10; Nehemiah 8:9; Ezekiel 44:23).

- To serve the priests (Numbers 18:4).

- To set up, dismantle, and transport the tabernacle (Numbers 10:17–21).

- To teach doctrine and administer justice (Deuteronomy 33:10).

The tribe of Levi was called to be the custodians of the tabernacle and to maintain the secrets of God. Sacrifices were brought to the priest and sins were confessed. The tribe of Levite knew all of the family secrets. They often knew who and why sin offerings were made. They also knew how to hide in the tabernacle. Psalmist declared, "For in the time of trouble he shall hide me in his pavilion: in the secret of his tabernacle shall he hide me; he shall set me up upon a rock" (Psalm 27:5).

Secret things belong to God. The Levitical priests were powerful because they knew the secrets of God and the secret faults of men. "The secret things belong unto the LORD our God: but those things which are revealed belong unto us and to our children for ever, that we may do all the words of this law" (Deuteronomy 29:29). God saw holiness within Levi's tribe and opted to extend the secret power to them so they could serve him. They became focused on their goals in life, which were to serve God and bless his name. "And I will set my tabernacle among you: and my soul shall not abhor you. And I will walk among you, and will be your God, and ye shall be my people. I am the Lord your God, which brought you forth out of the land of Egypt, that ye should not be their bondmen; and I have broken the bands of your yoke, and made you go upright" (Leviticus 26:11–13). The general functions of the Levical priests were as follows:

- They offered sacrifices (Leviticus 9).

- They taught the Law (Leviticus10:11).

- They maintained the tabernacle (Numbers 18:3).

- They functioned in the holy place (Exodus 30:7–10).

- They inspected unclean persons (Leviticus 13:14).

- They judged controversies (Deuteronomy 17:8–13).

- They collected taxes (Numbers18:21, 26; Hebrews 7:5).

POINTS TO PONDER

The Secret of Levi—Secret Relationships. Levi was the third son of Jacob and Leah. His name means, "joining". This chapter is about the power of secret relationships. Levi secretly *joined* himself to Simeon, his older brother, and they both committed mass murder. Levi is symbolic of people who are involved in secret relationships. Many people find it necessary to conceal their relationships, perhaps because they are scrutinized by society's status quo and feel forced to maintain secret relationships. People who are involved in an extra-martial affair may need to conceal their relationships, and others may hide their relationships with people who have a different religion or political point of view. Sometimes people act ambivalent towards each other, but you do not know who is connected with whom these days. Levi represents secret alliances, secret friendships, secret affairs, and secret covenants. Jacob prophesied that Levi and his family would also be "divided and scattered."

- Do not establish secret relationships with angry people. "Make no friendship with an angry man; and with a furious man thou shalt not go: Lest thou learn his ways, and get a snare to thy soul" (Proverbs 22:24-25).

- Be wary of keeping company with chronic complainers. They are angry wolves covered with sheepskin.

- "Be not deceived: evil communications corrupt good manners" (1 Corinthians 15:33).

- You do not know who is connected with whom or where someone's loyalty starts or ends. You do not know who is talking in secret.

- Having sex and having babies do not equal intimacy and relationship.

- Like any wife, Leah wanted to be connected with her husband.

- Leah desired a relationship so deeply that she named her third son "Levi," which means, "joining."

- It seemed as if Jacob and Leah's relationship was doomed from the beginning.

- Angry men are dangerous.

- Unlike women, angry men can enjoy sex. And for Jacob it was just that—sex!

- Leah gave her body to Jacob in secret to pacify his anger and to give hope to her dream.

- Women can feel a man's unspoken anger. Leah could not make a heart connection.

- When life evolves into a storm of persecution, it may be necessary to return to the place where you first experienced God.

- The conventional wisdom is that secret alliances are more conducive to war than public alliances because secret alliances cannot be deterred.

- The two sins at issue are a lack of self-control and an inability to reign in anger even when justified.

- "The secret things belong unto the LORD our God: but those things which are revealed belong unto us and to our

children for ever, that we may do all the words of this law"
(Deuteronomy 29:29).

In our modern day vernacular, before Levi was elevated to
priesthood, he behaved like gangster! However, Levi found a way to
connect himself with God. He found a position in God. His younger
brother, Judah, also appeared weak but found a way to connect with
God in a much richer way. Judah found a relationship with God
through praise! How did he learn to praise God? How did he turn
his life around? Let us look closer at Judah's journey.

CHAPTER 4

THE SECRET OF JUDAH

SECRET PRAISE

"Judah, thou art he whom thy brethren shall praise: thy hand shall be in the neck of thine enemies; thy father's children shall bow down before thee. Judah is a lion's whelp: from the prey, my son, thou art gone up: he stooped down, he couched as a lion, and as an old lion; who shall rouse him up? The scepter shall not depart from Judah, nor a lawgiver from between his feet, until Shiloh come; and unto him shall the gathering of the people be. Binding his foal unto the vine, and his ass's colt unto the choice vine; he washed his garments in wine, and his clothes in the blood of grapes: His eyes shall be red with wine, and his teeth white with milk." (Genesis 49:8–12).

This chapter is about secret praise. Have you ever tried singing, shouting, dancing, rejoicing, or praying to God in secret? God desires both public and private praise, but nothing transforms your mind and spirit like praising God in secret. Secret praise is the act of withdrawing to a place of solitude for the purpose of magnifying your connection with the Lord. The flesh is crucified in secrecy. The flesh hates solitude and hates to be silenced. Jesus said the flesh wants to be seen (Matthew 23:5). Praising God in secret starves the flesh of the "audience syndrome," recognition, pride, and accolades. Motives are purified in secrecy. Praising God in secret is the secret to achieving change. As we will see in this chapter, there is power in praying and praising God in secret.

On the day of Pentecost, the New Testament church was born. God gave the church a secret language for praise. This praise language is also called, glossolalia or, speaking in tongues. No human can understand this secret language. The language is a secret praise to God. Paul writes, "For he that speaketh in an unknown tongue speaketh not unto men, but unto God: for no man understandeth him; howbeit in the spirit he speaketh mysteries. But he that prophesieth speaketh unto men to edification, and exhortation, and comfort. He that speaketh in an unknown tongue edifieth himself; but he that prophesieth edifieth the church" (1 Corinthians 14:3-4).

This praise language was the initial sign that the church was born and alive. Let us consider the secret praise of Judah.

1) From denial to praise
2) The secret praise of Judah's brothers
3) Birthright and blessing
4) A lion's secret praise
5) The secret of the scepter
6) The secret of Shiloh

1) From denial to praise. "And she conceived again, and bare a son: and she said, Now will I praise the LORD: therefore she called his name Judah; and left bearing" (Genesis 29:35).

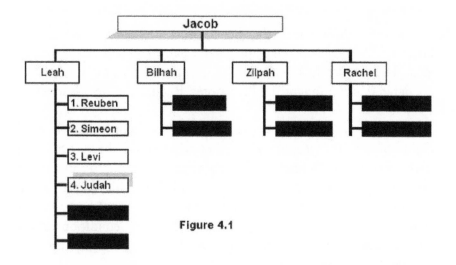

Figure 4.1

As shown in Figure. 4.1, Judah was the fourth son born of Jacob and Leah. When he was conceived, Leah said, "This time I will praise the Lord," and therefore she named him Judah (Genesis 29:35), which means, "praise." We have seen on three occasions how Leah tried to force her love on Jacob, but love can never be forced. Even though Leah had given Jacob three sons, his affection had not changed towards her. Forcing someone to love you is self-abuse. Leah is fearful of living a life without Jacob's love. She is fearful of failure. The fear of failure is also known as atychiphobia. Someone said, "The fear of failure is the father of failure." Her fear motivated her to produce babies (Reuben, Simeon, and Levi) in hopes of winning Jacob's love.

Daily talk shows are flooded with story lines of women who force their love on men. Oftentimes the men have made their feelings clear by not showing any interest in a committed relationship. Rather than accepting this position, some women secretly plan to seduce the men and become pregnant, thus forcing the men to be a part of their lives forever. This is a secret sin. Having a secret sin is like carrying a hundred-pound bag of rocks on your back. These women will forever be weaving a web of lies and trying to force a love that does not fit. If a woman wants to win a man, she must learn his secrets. She must learn his secret passions, desires, visions, and faults.

Genesis 29:30 tells us that Jacob loved Rachel more than Leah. Genesis 29:31 says that Jacob hated Leah. The word hate means Jacob loved Leah less than Rachel. Jacob's passion for Rachel was unchanged and unrelenting. He wanted Rachel and only Rachel.

Leah's secret praise process. Leah could no longer bear the dark nights of secretly weeping alone, but what could she do? She felt rejected and secretly grieved. Giving birth to her fourth son did not fill her empty heart—she wanted time with Jacob. She wanted a real relationship with him. She wanted his love. In the midst of Leah's chaos, what did it take to get to praise? In chaotic conditions, there are six steps to reaching praise. Let us examine this praise process, as shown in Figure 4.2.

Her denial. The first level of the praise process is denial. Leah refused to accept the fact that Jacob did not love her, and each night she cried in her secret place, "This cannot be happening to me!" She wanted companionship with Jacob. She was exhausted from rejection, and she had no psychiatrist or psychologist to call. No one understood her secret pain. She went to bed each night alone, denying the pain she felt. "I know he loves me," she exclaimed, "I

Figure 4.2- Praise Process

have given him many sons ... surely he loves me." Then she questioned, "Does he really love me or is it just the sex?" Leah was confused, and she found herself in a hard, secret place—a place of denial. From this hard place she moved from denial to anger.

Her anger. The second level of the praise process is anger. Leah was angry because of Jacob's rejection, and she became angry with her father, her husband, her sister, and her slave girl. Why was she so angry? Her father treated her as property, Jacob did not love her, and Rachel was favored. Leah felt as if not only the whole world had turned against her but the whole universe, including God.

Her bargaining. The third level of the praise process is bargaining. After experiencing anger, Leah attempted to bargain her way into Jacob's heart. She bargained with her body. "I will give you more babies if you give me love," she thought. Even after her seventh child, Jacob's heart still did not change.

Her depression. The fourth level of the praise process is depression. When bargaining, negotiating, and compromising does not work, depression sets in. Leah had created a mental prison for herself, exhausted by self-pity and unfulfilled wishes. Leah was consumed completely with trying to win the affections of a man who could not and would not reciprocate her love and secret longings. She was awakened mentally when she came to realize her self-torment must stop. The bitterness had to end for her to truly live. "Why did God allow me to suffer in this way?" she asked. She felt that everybody was against her, she had lost the love of her own husband (that she never had), and she was not able to understand the way in which God dealt with her. Every day she was reminded of Jacob as she saw the physical features (nose, eyes, feet, and hands) of Jacob in her children.

Her revelation. The fifth level of the praise process is a revelation from God. God had to speak to Leah in order for her to move from a place of depression to a place of revelation. God had to reveal his power and give her a song of deliverance. The psalmist declared, "Thou art my hiding place; thou shalt preserve me from trouble; thou shalt compass me about with songs of deliverance" (Psalm 32:7). Leah had to understand that God would preserve her from trouble.

Her acceptance. The sixth level of the praise process is acceptance. It is not until Leah reached Egypt that she accepted the revelation of God. She accepted the fact that Jacob would never love her as he loved Rachel. Our favorable acceptance of our conditions is a prerequisite to praise.

Her praise. The seventh level of the praise process is praise. "For his anger endureth but a moment; in his favour is life: weeping may endure for a night, but joy cometh in the morning" (Psalm 30:5). While in Egypt, Leah blossomed. She found joy in Egypt, she praised God, and she found a wealthy place. This wealthy place was a place of praise. As the psalmist declared, "Thou hast caused men to ride over our heads; we went through fire and through water: but thou broughtest us out into a wealthy place" (Psalm 66:12). This transition did not happen overnight, however. God assisted her in changing her focus, guiding her down the new path, and opening her mind to the love she previously had pushed aside for her worldly consumption of rejection.

End of "the blame and shame game." Yet, at the birth of Judah, Leah rose above her envy and rejection and got to the source of all blessing when she said, "I will praise the Lord." At the birth of Reuben, Leah asked Jacob, "Will you love me?" and he answered, "No!" (Shame on the devil!) At the birth of Simeon she asked Jacob, "Will you love me now?" He said, "No!" (Shame on Jacob.) At the birth of Levi she asked Jacob, "Will you please love me?" but he said no. (Shame on Leah). At the birth of Judah, Leah had apparently stopped naming her children to reflect her pain and the desire to win her husband. The love and longing in her heart had shifted. She was focused on God and on the need to praise Jehovah. She discovered that the remedy for fear and rejection was secret praise. Secret praise is therapeutic. "It is good for me that I have been afflicted; that I might learn thy statutes" (Psalm 119:71).

Judah saves Joseph. The Bible tells us quite a bit about Judah. Judah was mentioned in connection with the sale of his brother Joseph. Even though their mother learned the power of secret praise, it had not affected her sons. Satan did not care about her secret praise as long as it did not affect her sons' behavior. In Genesis 37, Joseph's brothers concocted a secret plan to kill him, but Judah came to the rescue and saved Joseph from death. Judah knew that blood could not be concealed and secret sins would not stay secret very long. Judah asked his brothers, "What profit is it if we slay our brother, and conceal his blood?" (Genesis 37:26). Rather than killing Joseph, Judah proposed that his riotous brothers sell Joseph into slavery. It was quick thinking on Judah's part to exploit his brothers' secret greed. He saved his brother from an angry mob. Their secret was that his brothers loved money more than they hated Joseph.

Paul writes to Timothy, "For the love of money is the root of all evil: which while some coveted after, they have erred from the faith, and pierced themselves through with many sorrows" (1 Timothy 6:10). Even some preachers and priests love money more than the ministry. Their prosperity in preaching and love for money is masked with fast-talking, motivational jargon, and twisted Scriptures. These preachers love to be seen on television, but in reality they love money more than their poor brothers who are trapped in financial pits.

2) The secret praise of Judah's brothers. "Judah, thou art he whom thy brethren shall praise: thy hand shall be in the neck of thine enemies; thy father's children shall bow down before thee" (Genesis 49:8).

Jacob was a man of faith, and he was looking forward to the future as he made his prophecies on the day that his sons would be initiated as the tribes of Israel. Jacob made three powerful statements to Judah. First, he declared Judah's brothers would praise him. Second, he stated that Judah would defeat his enemies. Third, Jacob said Judah would be the leader among his brothers. Why would Judah's brothers praise him? Judah had a tumultuous life and made lots of mistakes, yet he earned the respect and praise of his brothers. Let us look at Judah's portfolio.

- He abandoned his family (Genesis 38:1).

- He married an ungodly Canaanite woman against his father wishes (Genesis 38:2).

- He raised two wicked sons whom God killed because of their wickedness (Genesis 38:7-10).

- His wife died (Genesis 38:12).

- He was drawn to prostitution and illicit relationships, and he lacked self–control (Genesis 38:16).

- He impregnated Tamar, his daughter-in-law (Genesis 38:25-26).

- He was hypocritical and threatened to kill Tamar when he discovered she was pregnant (Genesis 38:24).

- He lied to Tamar (his daughter-in-law) by reneging on his promise to give her his third son in marriage (Genesis 38:11, 26).

Judah was his own greatest enemy. You must conquer the enemy within before you can do battle with the enemy without. Yet, Jacob prophesied on his deathbed that Judah's brothers would praise him. What turned Judah's circumstances around such that his brothers would praise him? Would he praise God so intensely that it would gain the respect of his brothers? No, Judah had a "prodigal son experience!" (Luke 15). "Prodigal" means "wasteful," and Judah was wasting his life away. However, like the prodigal son he turned his life around.

The prodigal son story is about repentance and forgiveness. Judah's lifestyle and behavior was all but dead, but his father saw that "he was alive and well." Judah's background was shady, but Jacob saw in him a clear future. Jacob, an old, blind man at the time of the prophecies, remembered how Judah had responded to a defining moment in his life when his secrets were exposed (Genesis 38:26).

From repentance to praise. Judah's defining moment came three months after Judah had an affair with Tamar, when someone (probably Simeon) told Judah that his daughter-in-law had been like a prostitute and was now pregnant. Judah ordered that Tamar be brought before him to be burned up.

When Tamar was brought, she said to Judah, "The man who has made me pregnant is the owner of these things" and then produced the signet, bracelets, and staff which belonged to Judah (Genesis 38:25). With that, Judah repented and acknowledged that the things were his. He praised her and said she was more righteous than he because he had not kept his promise. He had promised to give Tamar Shelah (his youngest son) to Tamar as a husband. Therefore, Tamar was judged innocent and spared. Judah was the guilty one. Tamar gave birth to twins, and their names were Pharez and Zarah.

Confession of Sin. Just imagine if Judah had denied having any contact with Tamar and proceeded to burn her. Luckily Judah did not respond that way. He experienced a transformation that would impact his destiny. Unlike his brother Reuben, Judah publicly acknowledged his scandalous relationship with Tamar. Judah "came to himself" and confessed his sin. He praised Tamar (Genesis 38:26) and declared her to be more righteous than he. He acknowledged that his behavior was unrighteous and pledged never to have another sexual encounter with Tamar. Genesis 38:26 states, "And Judah acknowledged them, and said, She hath been more righteous than I; because that I gave her not to Shelah my son. And he knew her again no more."

Repentance is powerful because in repentance we receive forgiveness and experience God's love for us. Judah then had a reason to praise God. He had been pardoned. He was free of condemnation, guilt, and evil secrets. True repentance always produces secret praise. Judah's blessing was connected to his repentant heart. Luke 13:5 reads, "Except ye repent, ye shall all likewise perish."

The secret of repentance. Repentance has several distinct steps. First, one must recognize one's sinful condition. Next, one must want to change their ways, confess their sin to God, and do a 180 degree turn away from their sin. Judah's repentant heart earned the praise of his brothers.

3) Birthright and blessing. 1 Chronicles 5:1–2 tells us that Reuben lost his birthright and blessing, as discussed in chapter one. The birthright and blessing were then divided among two other sons. Joseph received the birthright, but Judah received the blessing. The main thing is to get the blessing. The blessing is greater that the birthright. A birthright refers to a person's inheritance, but a blessing refers to dominion, happiness, prosperity and spiritual privilege. Remember, Esau's anger catapulted him to murder when Jacob stole his blessing. Esau seemed less bothered, however, when Jacob tricked him into selling his birthright.

Table 4.1, below, compares the birthright with the blessing. The birthright entitled Joseph to wealth, privilege, and power, and the blessing entitled Judah to salvation, forgiveness, communion with God, a heavenly place, obedience, anointing, healing, conversion, and power.

Joseph	Judah
Birthright	Blessing
A birthright is defined as something that parents pass on to their children. It refers to a right, privilege, or possession to which one is entitled by birth.	A blessing is defined as having God's favor upon you and within you. It refers to dominion, that is, one becomes the head of the extended family when the father dies.
The promise of future rewards that would come with the inheritance.	The promise of salvation, forgiveness, communion with God, heavenly place, anointing, healing, conversion, and power
Special inheritance, usually two-thirds of the family estate. (Deuteronomy 21:17).	God's good will and God's favor

Table 4.1

4) A lion's secret praise. "Judah is a lion's whelp: from the prey, my son, thou art gone up: he stooped down, he couched as a lion, and as an old lion; who shall rouse him up?" (Genesis 49:9).

The above scripture tells of Jacob's prophecy. He foretells that Judah will be a "lion's whelp" in the latter days. A whelp is another name for a young lion cub. Jacob prophesied that Judah would be a very young nation in the latter-day period of time. This perfectly describes the modern Israeli nation. The Israeli nation was "born" in the post World War II period. It is still a "young nation" in the world with a powerful voice. Even though enemies geographically surround the Israeli nation, it continues to roar with a voice of liberation. People with a clean heart can enjoy the benefits of Israel (Judah). The Psalmist declared "Truly God is good to Israel, even to such as are of a clean heart" (Psalm 73:1).

Jacob described Judah, as a lion who roars in the jungle. His roar is symbolic of believers' praise. For the believer, a lion's secret praise is calling on the name of Jesus. Calling on the name of Jesus causes devils to tremble. They are frightened by the power of his name. James 2:19 says, "Thou believest that there is one God; thou doest well: the devils also believe, and tremble." In Revelation 5:5, the Lord Jesus Christ is called, "the lion of the tribe of Judah," alluding to Jacob's prophecy (Genesis 49:10).

Jacob prophesied that Judah would be like a lion resting in secret, as he saw a crouching lion hiding in high grass when he looked at Judah. The full force of this cannot be understood unless we bear in mind that a lion or a lioness, when lying down after satisfying their hunger, will not attack anyone. The image was meant to represent Judah as calm and quiet yet still formidable.

Table 4.2 compares the characteristics of a lion with someone giving praise. The characteristics of a lion are manifest in the life and work of the Messiah. He will arrest every opposing force of Satan and establish his universal kingdom. Glory be to God—we will be with him and like him in the final overthrow of Satan's kingdom!

Characteristics of a lion	Characteristics of the secret praiser
Lions roar to establish their territory.	A believer praises to establish their freedom.
A lion's roar can be heard for more than five miles.	A believer's praise reaches eternity.
Lions mark their territories by means of scent deposits, necessitating a good sense of smell.	The sweet scent of a Praiser affects the atmosphere.
The lion represents strength, vigor, and courage. The lion is stronger than any other animal.	A believer's praise represents joy of the death, burial, and resurrection of Jesus. The believer knows that Jesus is stronger than any god or power.
The lion is the king of the beasts.	The Praiser knows Jesus as King of Kings and worthy of all praise.
The lion represents vigilance because it is believed to sleep with its eyes open.	The Praiser knows that Jesus sees everything. "Are not five sparrows sold for two farthings, and not one of them is forgotten before God?" (Luke 12:6).

Table 4.2

Jacob had no conception that nearly three thousand years would pass before his prophecy would or could be fulfilled, or that its fulfillment would involve the glorified Son of God.

5) The secret of the sceptre. "The sceptre shall not depart from Judah, nor a lawgiver from between his feet, until Shiloh come; and unto him shall the gathering of the people be" (Genesis 49:10).

Figure 4.3 is a picture of the sceptre. This sceptre was a long iron rod or spear with a U-shaped fork at one end, the points of both prongs being sharpened; the other end of the spear was pointed. The staff or rod represented authority or the right to rule. In a king's court, the king would have used the sceptre to represent a judgment. The sceptre represented power and praise.

- Power and praise would not depart from Judah. Judah's tongue became his scepter. "Death and life are in the power of the tongue: and they that love it shall eat the fruit thereof" (Proverbs 18:21). The word, "sceptre" is recorded over fifteen times in the Bible. Here are a few examples of its use:

- Symbolic of life as Esther approached the throne. "Then the king held out the golden sceptre toward Esther. So Esther arose, and stood before the king" (Esther 8:4).

- Symbolic of power as David exalted God. "Thy throne, O God, is for ever and ever: the sceptre of thy kingdom is a right scepter" (Psalm 45:6).

- Symbolic of the power of rulers. "The LORD hath broken the staff of the wicked, and the sceptre of the rulers" (Isaiah14:5).

- Symbolic of Christ being our sceptre of righteousness. Christ makes our praise righteous. He imputes power into our praise. "But unto the Son he saith, Thy throne, O God, is for ever and ever: a sceptre of righteousness is the sceptre of thy kingdom" (Hebrews 1:8).

The sceptre remained in the tribe of Judah until Christ came and gave us rest and peace. This is a remarkable prediction—that the Messiah could come, not from the line of the firstborn Reuben, but from the line of Judah, and that Judah would be the dominate tribe among the twelve right up until the One comes who alone has the right to hold the sceptre, who alone gives rest and peace.

Generational leaders. Jacob also prophesied that Judah's tribe would not lose its right to rule over itself. "Nor a lawgiver from between his feet" means his children or descendants would be leaders and lawgivers.

6) The secret of Shiloh. "The sceptre shall not depart from Judah, nor a lawgiver from between his feet, until Shiloh come; and unto him shall the gathering of the people be" (Genesis 49:10).

Angels desired to know the secrets of the Shiloh (1 Peter 1:12). Shiloh was the name of a place in Israel, but the meaning of its name has been revealed to Christians. The Hebrew word "Shiloh" signifies "he whose it is," or "that which belongs to him." The prophecy regarding Judah meant that the rulership would not depart from Judah until one comes to whom the rulership really belongs. At that time the rulership would depart from Judah. Shiloh signifies peace of mind, wholeness, completion or fullness, and represents the Prince of Peace, the Messiah or Savior. Jesus was a direct descendant of Judah, as recorded in the 1st chapter of Matthew. The name Judah applies to only one of the twelve tribes, but is often used to designate the Jewish nation as a whole.

POINTS TO PONDER

The Secret of Judah—Secret Praise. Judah was the fourth son of Jacob and Leah. His name means, "praise". Judah represents those people who understand the power of secret praise. Praising God in secret is therapeutic. Glossolalia (speaking in other tongues) is a form of secret praise. "He that speaketh in an unknown tongue edifieth himself; but he that prophesieth edifieth the church" (1 Corinthians 14:4). Jacob prophesied that Judah's family would display the characteristics of a lion.

- Jesus commanded us to pray in secret. "And when thou prayest, thou shalt not be as the hypocrites are: for they love to pray standing in the synagogues and in the corners of the streets, that they may be seen of men. Verily I say unto you, they have their reward. But thou, when thou prayest, enter into thy closet, and when thou hast shut thy door, pray to thy Father which is in secret; and thy Father which seeth in secret shall reward thee openly" (Matthew 6:5-6).

72

- Secret praise is the voluntary and temporary act of withdrawing to privacy for the purpose of magnifying the Lord.

- If a woman wants to win a man, she must learn his secrets. She must learn his secret passions, desires, visions, and faults.

- There is power in praying and praising God in secret.

- The remedy for rejection is secret praise. Secret praise is therapeutic.

- Satan does not care about your secret praise if it does not affect your behavior or the behavior of those connected to you.

- Your secret praise must be greater than your secret pain.

- Nothing transforms the mind like praising God in secret. The flesh is crucified in secret. It is starved of an audience, recognition, and accolades. Praising God in secret is the secret to change.

- Secret sins will not stay secret for very long.

- Secret sin is like carrying one hundred pounds of rocks on your back.

- Praising God in secret is spiritually synergistic.

- The fear of failure is the father of failure.

- "Death and life are in the power of the tongue: and they that love it shall eat the fruit thereof" (Proverbs 18:21).

Judah found a way to be thankful to God. But what happens when God appears distant and irrelevant in our lives? What happens when you feel God is unjust or worse non-existent? Dan was the first son of the maidservant. He did not have any praise for God. He did not like the way God handled His business. Why was he so perplexed with God's judgment and justice? Let us look closer at Dan's frustration and God's secret justice.

CHAPTER 5

THE SECRET OF DAN

SECRET JUDGMENT

"Dan shall be a serpent by the way, an adder in the path, that biteth the horse heels, so that his rider shall fall backward" (Genesis 49:17).

This chapter is about the secret justice of God. Some have said that secret justice is no justice at all. God is responsible for executing justice. It is a difficult thing for people to understand the justice of God. The very idea of God exceeds our reasoning and understanding. The Bible says vengeance belongs to God. "He will repay" (Deuteronomy 32:35).

The Old Testament definition of justice is that each person will get what he deserves. The law of "an eye for an eye" (Exodus 21:24) is called the law of retribution. The law of retribution states that the punishment should be like the injury. This is also called the law of equivalency. On the Day of Judgment, God will be responsible for ensuring that each punishment fits its crime. When the punishment is compatible with the crime, it is called justice.

Is there a penalty for rejecting God? What happens when a person rejects Him and nothing seems to happen? What happens when you do not see God executing his vengeance or justice? What happens when you do not see God repaying evil with evil? Why does God allow evil men to go free? Why does God allow godly men to suffer while ungodly men enjoy the pleasures of this world? Will God repay Adolph Hitler for the six millions Jews killed? Was the suicide bullet to Hitler's head sufficient to declare it to be justice? Will the Islamic terrorists, who killed in the name of God, be judged for their destructive acts in New York City or was the death of the terrorists in the burning plane that collapsed the Twin Towers sufficient justice?

God is a God of justice. Judgment Day is coming. He will sit on the throne. He has created hell to execute his justice. His justice is presently concealed but will be executed in public. Apostle Paul declared that one day we will see the total execution of God's justice. "Behold, he cometh with clouds; and every eye shall see him, and they also which pierced him: and all kindreds of the earth shall wail because of him. Even so, Amen" (Revelations 1:7). God's justice is not only to be feared but something to be hoped for.

A breach of God's justice? Let us consider several examples of secret justice. The death of Jesus on the cross at Calvary appeared to have been a breach of God's justice because an innocent man was killed. There were two things Jesus desired at Calvary. He wanted to hear the voice of God, and he did not want to feel abandoned by his father. Jesus was the most righteous man who ever lived. He was totally holy, perfect, and without sin. Why would God allow a righteous man to be forsaken? The righteous are never forsaken (Psalm 37:25). Only sinners die! Yet Jesus was crucified. Was this justice? Ezekiel 18:4 states, "The soul that sinneth, it shall die." The soul that does not sin does not die. Jesus never sinned but was condemed to death. Romans 6:23 states, "The wages of sin is death, but the gift of God is eternal life."

At about the ninth hour on Calvary, Jesus cried out in a loud voice, "Eloi, Eloi, lama sabachthani?" That means, "My God, my God, why have you forsaken me?" (Matthew 27:46 NIV). Was justice served when God abandoned Jesus on the cross? Jesus encountered there the secret justice of God. Every word of God is full of justice, yet for the first time Jesus failed to hear his father's voice of justice. Was the crucifixion of Jesus God's justice? It is not uncommon to see wicked people abandoned both by heaven and earth, but it is perplexing to see a righteous man seemingly abandoned by God. At Calvary, a holy man was made unholy in a matter of seconds. Jesus experienced a transformation from the epitome of sinlessness to the epitome of sinfulness. This gave God the right to execute his justice on Jesus, a righteous man who was made unrighteous so that we might become righteous like him (2 Corinthians 5:21).

Mary's justice - "Be it according to thy word." Mary, the mother of Jesus, watched her son bleed to death on a dirty cross. Nearly thirty-three years earlier, she had been visited by an angel. Mary was known for surrendering to the will of God, and when the angel delivered a command, Mary responded, "Behold the handmaid of the Lord; be it unto me according to thy word" (Luke 1:38). But as she watched her son crucified, could she still say, "Be it according to thy word?" Yes, she could! She understood the secret justice of God. Mary taught herself to trust in the sovereignty of God's Word and not to be shaken by incomprehensible acts of God. Let us review Mary's faith resume (see Luke 1).

- Mary was without fear when the angel Gabriel stood before her. Mary said to him, "Be it according to thy word."

- Mary was informed that as a virgin, she would become pregnant without a husband or even a man. Mary did not flinch. She responded, "Be it according to thy word."

- Mary was told by Gabriel that Jesus would "reign over the house of Jacob for ever, and of his kingdom there will be no end." Mary responded, "Be it according to thy word."

- Mary was told to name her child Jesus, which means, "salvation." I believe Mary's continued response was, "Be it according to thy word."

- Mary was told by Simeon that "a sword shall pierce your soul" and that secret thoughts would be revealed (Luke 2:35). I believe Mary's mindset was, "Be it according to thy word."

But at Calvary, though she did not utter those prophetic words, I believe her inner thoughts were, "Be it according to thy word." She was faced with a new level of mystery and secrecy of God's justice. Even Jesus could not hear or see God's justice. He was a sinner, separated from the voice of God. But Jesus declared at Gethsemane, "Not my will, but thine, be done" (Luke 22:42).

Job's justice -"Yet, will I trust in him." Another example of God's secret justice is seen in the case of a man named Job. In the book of Job another righteous man suffered for no apparent reason. This story revolves around the perplexing question of why the righteous suffer and how their suffering can be reconciled with the infinite goodness and holiness of God. Job lost his family, his wealth, and his health. He then sat "among the ashes," where he was visited by three friends who came to mourn with him and offer their explanations rather than comfort him in his misfortune.

Job's three friends attempted to explain the justice of God, implying that suffering was always the outcome of sin. Job desperately asserted his innocence. God appeared to hide himself in Job's dilemma. At times, Job appeared almost delirious under the unjust insinuations made by his three friends and bordered upon accusing God of injustice, but he recouped his confidence in divine goodness and protested that he would finally be vindicated and submit to the secret justice of God. "Though he slay me, yet will I trust in him: but I will maintain mine own ways before him" (Job 13:15).

The secret justice of God is when God delays the execution of his justice or we fail to see it because it is divinely hidden. As with the case of Job, we may be perplexed as to why God hid himself, yet behind apparent chaotic and senseless sufferings lie purpose and meaning.

The hidden justice of God. *Nelson's Illustrated Bible Dictionary* defines justice as the practice of what is right and just. Justice (or judgment) specifies what is right, not only as measured by a code of law but also by what makes for right relationships as well as harmony and peace. The secret justice of God is the concealment of his impartiality. It is the hidden scales of his justice. It is the execution of his righteousness behind the veils of secrecy. God executes vengeance in his own time. Though not fully understood, he demonstrates the highest practice of justice. His fairness to mankind is matchless. It is God's invisible poetic justice. It is God's uncommunicative balance of righteousness.

The secret justice of God does not mean his justice does not exist—it only means that his determinate counsel, foreknowledge, and eternal purposes have not yet been fully revealed. Paul writes, "But as it is written, Eye hath not seen, nor ear heard, neither have entered into the heart of man, the things which God hath prepared for them that love him. But God hath revealed them unto us by his Spirit: for the Spirit searcheth all things, yea, the deep things of God" (1 Corinthians 2:9–10). Therefore, the secret justice of God in history does not deny or contradict the manifested revelations of his justice.

"A measure of faith" for two modes of justice. There are two modes of God's justice, and both are part of the same, single purpose. This means God's justice is sometimes revealed and sometimes concealed. If you fail to see God's justice it does not mean God is not just, which is why God has given every human a measure of faith. God states that "the just shall live by faith."

So when we cannot explain the terrible inequalities and injustices of life, God gives us a measure of faith to trust in him and his secret justice. Paul wrote of how God gives a measure of faith to all men, saying, "For I say, through the grace given unto me, to every man that is among you, not to think of himself more highly than he ought to think; but to think soberly, according as God hath dealt to every man the measure of faith" (Romans 12:3).

If God is so good, why do good people suffer? This is a common question, but in order to answer it you must understand the secret justice of God. From very early in history men have been troubled by the terrible inequalities and injustices of life. The questions, "How could a good God make an awful world like this?" and "How could a holy God allow babies and innocent people to suffer with diseases and fall victim to senseless acts of terrorism?" are asked over and over again.

- Good people suffer because they live in a world of sin that has not yet been redeemed.

- Good people suffer because they try to live godly and Satan does not like it so he uses his tricks to afflict them.

- Good people suffer because it is a reminder that this world is not their home.

- Good people suffer because of the failures of their ancestors and countrymen.

The psalmist cried in despair for justice, saying, "Will the Lord cast off for ever? and will he be favourable no more? Is his mercy clean gone for ever? Doth his promise fail for evermore? Hath God forgotten to be gracious? Hath he in anger shut up his tender mercies? Selah" (Psalm 77:7–9). Sometimes God appears to hide himself from good people, but in truth he is always present.

While lying on his deathbed, Jacob turned his attention to his fifth son and declared, "Dan shall be a serpent by the way, an adder in the path, that biteth the horse heels, so that his rider shall fall backward" (Genesis 49:17). Lets consider the following issues relating to Dan.

1. Dan's secrets
2. Secrets of the serpents
3. The horses' heels
4. The fallen riders
5. The secret of waiting

1) Dan's secrets. With one foot in the grave, Jacob declared his fifth prophecy. His fifth son, Dan, would take on the characteristics of a serpent. Dan's dark secret was that he failed to see the justice of God and claimed, "God is unfair." It is dangerous to think God is unfair. An acid test of a Christian is trusting in God when you feel God has treated you unfairly. God is always fair, even when we fail to see his fairness.

Dan had ugly secrets. Dan is the first tribe of Israel to apostatize. Apostasy means to "fall away." A person who embraces truth but later embraces another gospel has committed apostasy. Many theologians believe that the Antichrist will come from the tribe of Dan. Dan means "justice" or "judgment." Dan is silent in Scripture and never utters a word. Your words, like his, may remain secret and silent, but your actions will reveal them.

There are five reasons why Dan could have felt God was unfair. Dan's life was seemingly full of injustices. First, justice was not served when his brother (Reuben) allegedly raped his mother. The whole matter was swept under the carpet and only exposed on Jacob's deathbed. Second, the treatment of his mother (Bilhah) was a miscarriage of justice. His mother was a "baby machine" and a "worthless pawn" for Rachel and Jacob, and no love or appreciation was ever expressed toward her. Third, a father that was connected with Jehovah God treated him like an unwanted son. His father had always seen him as a snake. Fourth, whenever they traveled he was positioned at the tail end of the procession. Fifth, Dan thought it was undeserving and improper to be the last in the family to offer sacrifices to Jehovah.

Sex rears its ugly head again! The Old Testament has many stories with sexual themes. The book of Genesis itself has more than thirty stories that deal with sexual issues. Even though Dan did not face any sexual issues, he must have felt injustice because his brother was not reprimanded for his sexual indiscretion with his mother. It was unfair that justice was not executed upon Reuben. The roots of sexual secrecy are planted very deeply. Generational curses are often sexually related issues and are often tied to ugly family secrets. As described in chapter one, Reuben had a sexual affair with Dan's mother, Bilhah. Was it consensual sex? Was it rape? Drawing lines between incest, adultery, and rape can be complex. Reuben was caught sleeping in Jacob's bed with Bilhah (Genesis 35:22). "And it came to pass, when Israel dwelt in that land, that Reuben went and lay with Bilhah, his father's concubine." Nothing was done to Reuben for this egregious act!

Dead from the neck up. I believe Dan felt it was unfair that his mother was not the wife of Jacob. Dan's mother was a slave of Rachel's and a concubine of Jacob's. A concubine is a woman who performs the sexual duties of a wife without being married to the man. Dan must have developed an inferiority complex because of Bilhah's physical enslavement. Throughout the Scriptures, Jacob never expressed love for Bilhah. Dan thought, "How unfair of you to treat my mother that way … you man of God!" Jacob loved Rachel and never asked for a blended family. He only desired one wife. Leah was cultural baggage, and Bilhah was baggage of a sort too. Imagine Jacob introducing both sisters at a dinner party. He would say something like, "This is my wife Rachel, and this is her sister Leah ... and the girl over there is Bilhah, Rachel's slave-girl." Slavery can never be justified. As Dan witnessed his mother's inferior treatment, I can hear him angrily question, "Where is God?"

Circumstances beyond Dan's control. As shown in Figure 5.2, Dan's mother was Bilhah. He was the first son of the maidservant. It was not Dan's choice to be raised in a blended family. Becnel's definition[8] of a Blended Family is --- "any marriage in which at least one of the spouses becomes a stepparent (new parent), regardless of the age of the children." There are unique challenges in a blended family. As we will see with Jacob, a parent and stepparent do not treat children in the blended family equally. Justice is not always served. Many stepparents find it difficult to love their stepchild or stepchildren. Discipline from a stepparent usually results in frustration, opposition, and disrespect. I believe Dan's life was full of challenges and that he always felt last or left out.

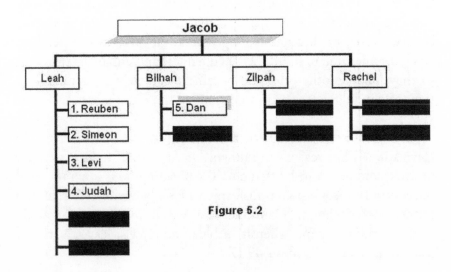

Figure 5.2

---

[8]   Becnel, Barbara Cottman, *The Co-Dependent Parent: Free Yourself by Freeing Your Child, 1st HarperCollins, pbk. Ed, July 1991.*

The open secret. It was not a secret that Dan was always last. The tribe of Dan marched from rear, or the far north side, of the tabernacle (Numbers 2:25). Thus, Dan was withdrawn as a boy, a follower standing in the shadows of his brothers. He was last to engage and conquer Israel's enemies.

The last son to worship. The Old Testament describes the meticulous process by which each tribe offered sacrifices to God. Again, Dan was assigned the last position to offer sacrifices unto Jehovah, and the tribe of Dan was the first tribe of Israel to plunge into pagan idolatry! Over the centuries, they became steeped in idolatry and image worship. They were slow to repent of their sins and come out of the prevalent end-time idolatry.

Pride clouds judgement. The tribe of Dan was indeed quite self-indulgent. The tribe of Dan as a whole was guilty of gross idolatry—even to the point of stealing the idols they used to practice their religion (Judges 18:14-31). They were also impatient and unwise, and they began to think less and less of God and the ways they were taught. They wanted a new, passive way to live without consequences. In Judges 18:30, the Danites set up some idols. They wanted to worship beauty, so they made a statue of a goddess and gave her a name. They wanted something to signify sexual openness and unbiblical relations, so they made another idol and became completely consumed with their self-indulgence. Their pride clouded their judgment.

Dan's name is left out of the sealing of the twelve tribes in Revelation 7. For reasons unknown, Dan is cut off from his twelve brothers and his name blotted out. The presumptuous ignorance and rejection of God's justice transformed Dan's behavior into that of a snake. Jacob declared, "Dan shall be a serpent by the way, an adder in the path, a serpent, when it slithers and crawls, leaves a trail or track in the sand" (Genesis 49:17).

2) Secrets of the serpents.

A need to blink. Jacob looked into the eyes of Dan and called him a serpent. Serpents (snakes) do not have eyelids and never blink. Dan never closed his eyes to contemplate, having already made his judgment and locked a stare on his prey. Snakes have clear membranes that cover their eyes, and their eyes are always open, even when they sleep. They do not blink when they look at their prey. This may be where the story that snakes hypnotize their prey comes from, though snakes cannot actually hypnotize anything. Jesus called the religious establishment of that day snakes too. They attempted to hypnotize people with the religiosity and traditions of men. Jesus cried out, "O generation of vipers how can ye, being evil, speak good things? for out of the abundance of the heart the mouth speaketh" (Matthew 12:34).

Camouflage experts. Jacob said Dan would pretend to be something he was not. He would pretend to be religious, righteous, and thirsty for God. Snakes use their coloration to hide—they are camouflage experts. Solid brown or gray snakes lie on the forest floor partly covered by leaves. Snakes are also decorated with spots and blotches to blend in with their surroundings, making them hard to see. Many snakes lie in ambush, sometimes for weeks, waiting for their prey to show up.

Secret of his venom. Jacob calls Dan a snake because his words would be venomous. Some snakes, such as the viper and cobra, kill with venom. When they bite, venom flows from their fangs into their prey's body through the wound the fangs made. Only poisonous snakes have fangs and venom glands. The fangs are similar to two hypodermic needles and may be shed and grow back several times a year. A single bite from a cobra can kill a large elephant. There is also enough venom in one cobra bite to kill ten to thirteen humans. The devil injected his mortal virus into the human race. Jesus came to heal us from the fatal bite of sin.

A deaf man's secret. Jacob called Dan a serpent because of his challenges to hear the truth. Snakes lack an outer ear opening. However, they have inner ears and can hear a limited range of sound carried on the air. Certain bones in a snake's head respond to sound waves and transmit them into the inner ear.

Snakes cannot be rewarded. Jacob called Dan a serpent because serpents cannot be trained or taught. Researchers have found it difficult to test the intelligence of snakes. Snakes are hard to train partly because they have irregular feeding habits and thus cannot be rewarded easily with food for performing correctly. They show little inclination to learn human tricks.

3) The horses' heels.

The snake that bit the horse. Jacob declared that Dan would "bite the horses' heels." In Scripture a horse is a symbol of freedom, strength, and power. Jacob prophesied that Dan would strike a person, a system, or a government that was in power. Notice Dan did not attack footmen but the man who was in a more dominant position. There are two things we should consider regarding the serpents bite. Where he bites and why he bites.

Where he bites. Jacob gives us quite a bit of detail here. He did not tell us that Dan simply bites the horse but tells us where he bites the horse. He bites the horse in its most vulnerable place—the heel. Notice the horse was not bitten on the leg, thigh, or stomach. The serpent found the secret weakness of the horse—the horse's Achilles heel. The term, implying a weak spot or flaw, comes from a Greek legend where the mother of the Greek hero Achilles holds him by the heels and dips him in the River Styx so that he would be invulnerable. However, his heels remained unprotected, and he was eventually killed by an arrow which pierced his heels. From this Greek legend, the phrase Achilles Heels has come to mean a weak spot or flaw. Jacob prophesied that Dan would find the secret weak spot of a dominant system or government. Remember the saying, "If you lose one nail, you lose the horseshoe, then a horse, then an army, and finally the kingdom."

Why he bites. Jacob did not tell us why the serpent bites but that the bite is unprovoked.

"Dan shall be a serpent by the way, an adder in the path, that biteth the horse heels, so that his rider shall fall backward" (Genesis 49:17).

4) The fallen riders

The rider's fall. It is interesting to hear that the rider was not bitten but the horse. The power, the system, and the government that carried the rider were attacked. Satan does not directly attack the soul but rather attacks those things that sustain the soul. Jacob said the serpent's bite would create a chain reaction. The serpent's bite would be so intense that the rider would fall backward. Let us consider three riders who fell backwards.

Samson. Samson, who was a judge from the tribe of Dan, fell because he could not keep a secret. When Samson began an affair with a woman name Delilah, the Philistines saw an opportunity to learn the secrets of Samson's strength. They offered Delilah a fortune to discover the secret and convey it to them. Samson told Delilah his secret.

Eve. Eve fell because she desired to know the secrets of God. Eve was the first woman. She was made by God from Adam's flesh. When the serpent came on the scene and spoke to Eve, he persuaded her that God was keeping a secret from her. "For God knows that in the day you eat of [the tree of knowledge of good and evil] your eyes will be open and you will be like God, knowing good and evil (Genesis 3:4-5).

Ananais and Sapphira. Ananais and Sapphira fell when they kept the profits from the property they sold. They had promised to give the profits from the land to the Church. The profit they received for the property far exceeded their expectations, and they decided to keep a large portion of it. Ananais and Sapphira lied to the apostles, telling them they only received a very small profit for the land. Their secret was exposed and God struck them dead (Act 5:1–12).

5) The secret of waiting.

It is to be noted that after Jacob had completed his prophecy concerning Dan in Genesis 49:17, he looked into Dan's eyes and saw the serpent. He saw the devil's face, and he saw the first of the tribes that would fall into idolatry. Having spoken of Dan as "a serpent by the way," Jacob recalled, perhaps by the will of the Holy Spirit, the words spoken by God to that old serpent the devil, as recorded in Genesis 3:15. The eyes of the dying patriarch looked beyond the serpent in Dan's eyes to the one who shall yet "bruise his head" and therefore said, "I have waited for Thy salvation, O Lord." (Genesis 49:18)

Jacob stated, "I have waited for the salvation of God." It is hard to wait. The Bible says, "The Lord is good to those who wait for Him, to the soul who seeks Him" (Lamentations 3:25 NKJV). Sometimes it is difficult to wait on God's answers and timing for the things that we want or need. Waiting on God is perhaps the most difficult thing to do as a Christian—it takes great faith. When you are hoping and praying for God to fulfill a promise and it does not become a reality soon enough, it can cause you to question the fairness or justice of God. Below is a list of biblical characters that waited on God.

- Abraham waited twenty-five years for God to fulfil his promise of a son.

- Joseph waited thirteen years in prison before his promotion.

- Moses waited forty years in the wilderness before his promotion.

- Noah waited one hundred twenty years for it to rain.

- Jacob waited fourteen years to marry Rachel.

- David waited fifteen years after Samuel anointed him before he became king of Israel.

- Jeremiah waited fifteen years after being called to preach before he uttered his first prophecy.

- Jesus waited thirty years before he started his ministry.

- Paul waited three years before he started to preach the gospel.

God had a plan for each of the individuals listed above. Let me encourage you by saying that God has plans for you. You must learn to wait. "For the vision is yet for an appointed time, but at the end it shall speak, and not lie: though it tarry, wait for it; because it will surely come, it will not tarry" (Habakkuk 2:3). .

POINTS TO PONDER

The Secret of Dan—Secret Judgment. Dan was the fifth son of Jacob. His name means "judging". Jacob prophesied that Dan and his family would display the characteristics of a snake. His mother's name was Bilhah. Dan represents the secret retaliation and the judgment of God. The tribes of Dan and Reuben were the first tribes to turn away from God. It is a secret how and when God will punish the wicked, but all will stand before the judgment seat of God. How will God judge? Will evil people really pay for their evil deeds? "Vengeance belongs to God" (Romans 12:19).

- Some have said that secret justice is no justice at all.

- God is responsible for executing justice.

- The law of "an eye for an eye" is usually called the law of retribution.

- On the cross, Jesus (a sinless man) struggled with the secret justice of God.

- Mary taught herself to trust in the sovereignty of God and to not be shaken by the incomprehensible acts that God allows.

- Although Job was perplexed as to why God hid himself, he knew beyond his apparent chaotic and senseless sufferings there was purpose and meaning.

- The secret justice of God is the concealment of his impartiality.

- God's fairness to mankind is matchless and incomprehensible.

- God's justice is sometimes revealed and sometimes concealed.

- It is dangerous to think God is unfair.

- Your words may remain secret and silent, but your actions will reveal them.

- Without faith it is impossible to understand God's justice.

- Jacob called Dan a serpent. Serpents cannot be trained.

- Waiting on God is perhaps the most difficult thing to do as a Christian, but God gives us faith to wait.

Dan secretly wrestled with theological issues. He could not understand God's justice. But his younger brother Naphtali also wrestled with issues of life, but was able to find liberty. Let us look closer at Naphtali's secret wrestling.

CHAPTER 6

THE SECRET OF NAPHTALI

SECRET WRESTLING

"Naphtali is a hind let loose: he giveth goodly words" (Genesis 49:21).

This chapter is about secret struggles. Nothing comes easy in life. Everyone struggles with something. The anatomy of a stuggle is very interesting. There are three stages to a struggle—the beginning, the middle, and the end, and everyone is always in one of these stages. Where are you with your struggle? Are you just starting to struggle with something? Are you in the middle of a struggle or just coming out of one?

Webster's Dictionary defines struggle as follows: "to contend with an adversary or opposing force, to advance with violent effort (like walking through snow), or to war, to fight, conflict of any kind or to task to achieve a goal." Anything or anyone that feels tied up struggles to be free. From the very beginning of our universe God's creation has struggled (Romans 8:23). Angels struggled in the heavens (Jude 6). Darkness struggled with light (John 1:5). Man struggled with obedience to God (Roman 5:19). Everything struggles. Even a small blade of grass must struggle for sunlight and rain. Why are there so many struggles?

Figure 6.1 shows two men wrestling. One man is struggling to get free. We are attracted to such contests. Struggles are entertaining, sometimes. We enjoy public struggles and fights. We spend many hours in front of television screens watching sports teams and individuals struggle for victory.

Figure 6.1

Why do people struggle? People struggle because they feel trapped, and traps are being set everyday. Who is setting these traps -- wicked men, demons, and people who are envious and jealous. Psalm 10:9 speaks of wicked men who wait in secret to destroy the poor, saying, "He lieth in wait secretly as a lion in his den: he lieth in wait to catch the poor: he doth catch the poor, when he draweth him into his net."

Jesus made himself accessible to people who felt trapped. No one likes feeling trapped by anyone or anything. Have you ever felt trapped? Have you ever told someone that you felt trapped? Many people find it embarrassing to publicly announce that they feel trapped. It is shameful and not politically correct to say, "I am trapped." Whether you are trapped in a marriage, a religious denomination, or a community, it is an unpleasant situation. When we get trapped, we struggle to get free and conceal our entrapments. We secretly wrestle for liberation. We want to be free, so we litigate and arbitrate for reasonable settlements to gain freedom.

In American culture, people who get trapped are perceived as weak. Criminals get trapped. Liars get trapped. Thieves get trapped. The misinformed get trapped. Lazy people get trapped. People who fail to do their homework get trapped. People who fail to read the fine print in contracts get trapped. Preachers, politicians, actors, and other public figures are known for getting trapped. They get trapped in adulterous relationships or by making unethical decisions.

King Solomon wrote that men are vulnerable and can easily be trapped by evil times. Ecclesiastes 9:12 (NIV) reads, "Moreover, no man knows when his hour will come: As fish are caught in a cruel net, or birds are taken in a snare, so men are trapped by evil times that fall unexpectedly upon them." We frequently see marriages that publicly appear to be happy and healthy but somehow suddenly dissolve. We later learn that "the happy marriage" was a mask and both spouses felt trapped and miserable.

We have also heard of pastors who appeared satisfied with their church and ministry and unexpectedly resigned from their positions. Again, we later learn of the pastor's secret struggles and his frustrations of being trapped by his deacon board or congregation.

Jesus tells a story of a man who has two sons who both felt trapped. The story is found in Luke 15:11–32. The younger brother was unhappy with living with his father—he felt trapped. How long had he been unhappy? He demanded his share of his inheritance while his father was still living, and then went off to a distant country where he "wasted his substance with riotous living" and eventually had to take work as a swine herder. There he felt trapped again and came to his senses. He determined to return home and throw himself on his father's mercy, and when he returned home his father greeted him with open arms. The father did not want his son to feel trapped but loved, so he gave him a chance to express his repentance. The father even killed a "fatted calf" to celebrate his son's return.

However, the older brother then became jealous and felt secretly trapped by the favored treatment of his faithless brother, and he was upset at the lack of reward for his own faithfulness.

It can be frightening to feel secretly trapped. Are you trapped in your marriage, your position or your job, your church, your ministry, your in-laws and stepchildren, financial debt, obesity, doctrinal points of view, or a boring and unfulfilled life? The list goes on and on. Sadly, many people feel that their lives are being wasted. They feel imprisoned in core areas of their lives.

Wrestling in the spirit. Each day the Christian believer is engaged in spiritual warfare. However, God provided the believer with a weapon to fight back. It is only our spiritual armor and the grace of God that enables us to overcome spiritual warfare. "For we wrestle not against flesh and blood, but against principalities, against powers, against the rulers of the darkness of this world, against spiritual wickedness in high places" (Ephesians 6:12).

People who feel trapped are restless. Are you restless? Are you spending your lifetime secretly wrestling for freedom? Jesus came into the world to save people who are restless and trapped. Jesus said, "Come unto me, all ye that labour and are heavy laden, and I will give you rest. Take my yoke upon you, and learn of me; for I am meek and lowly in heart: and ye shall find rest unto your souls. For my yoke is easy, and my burden is light" (Matthew 11:28–30).

A secret bone of contention. A friend of mine was engaged to marry a young lady after dating her for two years. But he realized that he did not love her and was not interested in maintaining a relationship with her. There were lots of things he did not like about his fiancé, but he kept his dissatisfactions and bones of contention a secret. He was frightened to break off the relationship for fear of his fiancé's response. She had threatened to kill herself if he left her. He felt guilty and responsible for her heartbreak, and he thought she *really* would commit suicide if he dissolved the relationship. He said he felt trapped, so in order to escape from the relationship he abruptly resigned from a lucrative computer job and moved out of state. His fiancé' never committed suicide. My friend told me he left because he just could not deal with the struggle. He was tired of wrestling with a dead-end relationship. My friend never found freedom, so he escaped to another state. However, Naphtali, the sixth son of Jacob never surrendered to his secret wrestlings. He fought his secret battles until he found freedom.

Now, let us turn our attention towards Naphtali, the sixth son of Jacob. As Naphtali stood beside his father's deathbed, Jacob said, "Naphtali is a hind let loose: he giveth goodly words" (Genesis 49:21). Here Jacob spoke poetically and prophetically. In this chapter we will consider Naphtali's secret struggles and the things which caused him to struggle. As we analyze the things Naphtali wrestled with, we will consider the following factors:

1) Family struggles
2) The secrets of the hind
3) The secret of bondage
4) Breaking the chains of Oppression
5) The secret of liberty

1) Family struggles. Naphtali's family was full of struggles. Naphtali's father (Jacob) struggled with his past and future. Naphtali's adopted mother (Rachel) struggled with Leah. Leah struggled with Jacob. His birth mother (Bilhah) struggled with Rachel. Even Naphtali's grandfather (Isaac) lived a life full of struggles.

Rachel's struggles. Rachel screamed at Jacob, "Give me children, or else I die" (Genesis 30:1). In desperation and despair, Rachel took her slave girl (Bilhah) and commanded her to sleep with her husband a second time. The Bible tells us that Rachel envied her sister Leah because Leah was able to give Jacob sons. "And when Rachel saw that she bare Jacob no children, Rachel envied her sister; and said unto Jacob, "Give me children, or else I die" (Genesis 30:1). Jacob responded, "I am not God. I cannot cause you to become pregnant."

Nevertheless, Rachel ordered Bilhah to sleep with Jacob, and so Bilhah gave birth to a second son.

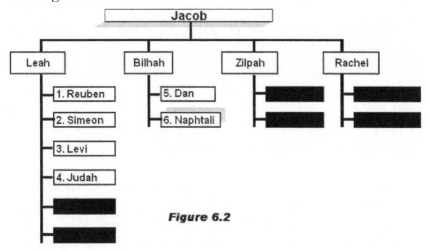

Figure 6.2

Rachel named him Naphtali because of her struggle with her sister and her inability to give birth. The name Naphtali means "wrestling." Bilhah had no choice but to accept the name because she was a slave. "And Rachel said, 'With great wrestlings have I wrestled with my sister, and I have prevailed': and she called his name Naphtali" (Genesis 30:8). The best inheritance parents can leave a child is a good name.

Bilhah's struggles. Bilhah, the slave girl, gave birth to two sons—Dan and Naphtali. As shown in Figure 6.2, Naphtali was her second son. Rachel took both sons, however, and throughout Scripture Bilhah was silent. She never spoke. I am sure she had lots to say about her circumstances. Rachel had authority over Bilhah's babies even though she was not the maternal mother. In spite of Rachel's shouts of victory that God had given her a son, the silent Bilhah knew who Naphtali really belonged to. Bilhah, the maid-slave, struggled in silence.

Leah's struggles. Leah struggled with a cold, insensitive husband. She struggled with her useless and ineffective strategies to win his love. She had given birth to four sons, and yet Jacob had no affection for her. Leah struggled with Jacob's inattention and lack of affection towards her.

Naphtali's struggles. Naphtali was born into a blended family full of secrets, challenges, and struggles. As a small boy, Naphtali saw his father's struggles and how it affected him. His father struggled with fear, guilt, and shame. Jacob was always fearful that his brother Esau would show up one day to keep his promise to kill him, and every day Naphtali saw the fear in his father's face. He saw his father struggle with the uncertainty of his future.

Esau's struggles. Esau was a great hunter and a man of his word. He vowed to kill Jacob (Genesis 27:41), and whatever Esau promised to do, he completed. Esau struggled with forgiveness. How could he ever forgive his brother? Jacob stole his birthright and his blessing. Jacob stole his identity and Esau swore to kill him. However, when Esau met Jacob about twenty years after he had promised to kill him, Esau kissed him and told him how much he really loved him. Esau had experienced secret healing. Secret healing is when God slowly removes the pains of the past in exchange for reconciliation.

Jacob's six struggles. The life of Naphtali's father was full of emotional, mental, and physical struggles. From birth, Jacob was always wrestling or struggling with something. Let us consider six things Jacob wrestled with. The first evidence of Jacob's struggles was during Rebekah's pregnancy, as he grabbed the heel of Esau while in his mother's womb (Genesis 25:26). Second, he wrestled with Esau (using a pot of porridge) to steal his blessing (Genesis 25:30). Third, he wrestled with Esau to steal his birthright (Genesis 27:21-24). Fourth, he wrestled with being tricked into marrying a woman he did not love (Genesis 29:25) Fifth, he wrestled with his uncle, who changed his salary ten times (Genesis 31:41). Sixth, he wrestled with an angel at Peniel and said to the angel, "I will not stop wrestling with you until you bless me." (Genesis 32:24). After each struggle, Jacob grew to become a better person. After each struggle he learned how to trust God. From Jacob's struggle we learn that how we react to a struggle can be more important than how we resolve a struggle.

Isaac's struggles. The life of Naphtali's grandfather, Isaac, was plagued with struggles. Genesis 26 tells two accounts of Isaac's struggles. Isaac struggled with the Philistines over the well in Esek, (Genesis 26:20) and he struggled over the well Sitnah. (Genesis 26:21) His struggles ended at Rehoboth. He struggled until God said you will no longer struggle. "And he removed from thence, and digged another well; and for that they strove not: and he called the name of it Rehoboth; and he said, For now the LORD hath made room for us, and we shall be fruitful in the land." (Genesis 26:22).

2) The secrets of the hind. Jacob looked into the eyes of Naphtali and called him a "hind." He did not call him a lion, wolf, or serpent. "Naphtali shall be a hind ..." A hind is a female deer. Naphtali and his tribe would reflect the characteristics of a deer. Let us consider the deer-like characteristics that were ascribed to Naphtali.

His feet. Jacob prophesied Naphtali would be like a deer and his feet would be like a deer's hoof. Naphtali would one day possess conqueror's feet and be able to declare, "He maketh my feet like hind's feet, and setteth me upon my high places" (Psalm 18:33).

As shown in Figure 6.3, deer are cloven-hoofed animals and have four hoofs, each with two large toes. Deer hoofs dig into the ground for sure footing, and they are also sharp enough to stomp on and slash an enemy. The most common sign

Figure 6.3

that deer leave behind are their heart-shaped hoofprints. The word "hind" is referenced ten times in the Bible. The word is generally used in a favorable context, as God used the phrase "hind's feet" to convey thoughts of sure-footedness, power and finesse. Let us review a few of these verses:

- **In the midst of struggles, God gives sure-footedness**. "He maketh my feet like hinds' feet: and setteth me upon my high places" (2 Samuel 22:34).

- **God displayed his glory at the birth of a calf.** "Knowest thou the time when the wild goats of the rock bring forth? or canst thou mark when the hinds do calve?" (Job 39:1).

- **God's word makes deer give birth**. "The voice of the LORD maketh the hinds to calve, and discovereth the forests: and in his temple doth every one speak of his glory" (Psalm 29:9).

- **The deer is smooth.** The woman in the book of Solomon adjured her audience to be as smooth as deer while her lover slept. "I charge you, O ye daughters of Jerusalem, by the roes, and by the hinds of the field, that ye stir not up, nor awake my love, till he please" (Song of Solomon 3:5).

His eyes. Jacob called Naphtali a deer because he would have great vision. He would have eyes like a deer. A deer's large eyes provide a wide field of view with binocular vision. Deer are virtually color-blind, but they can see shapes sharply and clearly and can detect the slightest movement. Naphtali was always ready to wrestle because he saw the secret things of God. Jesus said, "For judgment I am come into the world, that they which see not might see; and they that see might be made blind" (John 9:39). He would never experience blindness.

His ears. Jacob foresaw that Naphtali's ears would be like a deer's. A deer can swivel each of its ears around on its head to listen in two directions at once. Naphtali would be a tribe of faith. He would hear "goodly words" in his soul, and he would hear the quiet, small voice of God. "Faith comes by hearing the word of God." (Romans 10:17).

His speed. Jacob prophesied that Naphtali would be strong. With a top speed of thirty-six miles per hour, a mature deer can outrun any predator. A deer on the run can leap obstacles eight feet high. When closely pursued, deer zig, zag, and circle at full speed.

But deer are not perfect. They trip and slip and tumble and fall. They get stuck in deep snow and mud. Naphtali would get tangled but somehow get loose. He would travel at top speeds shouting a "good word." His goodly word would be, "I am free! Free from the power of sin! Free from the penalty of sin! Free from the presence of sin!"

3) The secret of bondage. Jacob understood that Naphtali would be in bondage for many years. It was secret bondage, because in public Naphtali smiled, said the right things, and dressed the right way. No one knew (except for Jacob) that he would be a son in bondage. Are you concealing your bondage? Are you hiding your pain? Are you suppressing your struggles? Jacob declared that, "Naphtali is a hind let loose." This verse suggests that Naphtali would be in bondage but would be free in the future. What did Naphtali struggle with? He struggled with the lust of the flesh, the lust eye, and the pride of life (1 John 2:16).

Jacob foresaw that Naphtali would be bound by his lust and the curse of the law. Jacob foresaw that the tribe of Naphtali would become slaves in Egypt and Babylon, and they would be bound in slavery for four hundred years and in captivity for forty years. Bilhah's servitude caused Naphtali mental bondage as he struggled with her circumstances. He also struggled with his faith, his finances, and his spirit.

4) Breaking the Chains of Oppression.

Goodly words. He gave "goodly words." Let us consider seven reasons why Naphtali would give "goodly words." First, his "goodly words" were an outgrowth of his faith. Second, he would tell of his personal experiences of being in slavery and captivity. He would share his secret scars and secret pains and tell how he was loosed from bondage and emancipated. Third, he would recount his blessings.

Naphtali was free from poverty because his brother Joseph was the viceroy of Egypt. Fourth, he would not be able to withhold his testimony—the word in his heart was irrepressible. Fifth, like the prophet Jeremiah, his testimony would burst forth from an inward fire. Sixth, Naphtali would give "goodly words" because it was his everyday duty. Seventh, he would give "goodly words" because the Holy Spirit inspired him.

Trapped and then Loosed! "Naphtali is a hind let loose: he giveth goodly words" (Genesis 49:21). Scripture suggests that Naphtali's character would be like a deer that was trapped and then let loose. Jacob prophesied that he would be set free like a mountain deer from the secret chains of sin and condemnation (Genesis 49:21). Like a deer which has been set free from a trap, Naphtali moved from being the quiet one to a teacher of wisdom, for "he giveth goodly words." Naphtali had a testimony and told his secret. He gave words of encouragement, and his words were pleasant.

"Pleasant words are as honeycomb, sweet to the soul, and health to the bones" (Proverbs 16:24). Naphtail's mind had been redeemed. He could not stop talking about his new freedom. Scripture says, "Let the redeemed of the LORD say so, whom he hath redeemed from the hand of the enemy" (Psalm 107:2). Naphtali's "goodly words" were his testimony of his freedom. His thoughts and words were pure. "The thoughts of the wicked are an abomination to the LORD: but the words of the pure are pleasant words" (Proverbs 15:26).

5) The secret of liberty. We are told by the prophet Hosea (Hosea 12:4) how Jacob wrestled with an angel until he found liberty. Prayers, tears and faith were his weapons. Prayer is the secret to liberty. Jacob's secret prayer was fervent and effective. As Apostle James writes, "Confess your faults one to another, and pray one for another, that ye may be healed. The effectual fervent prayer of a righteous man availeth much" (James 5:16). Prayer is not only a physical discipline but a spiritual discipline. Jacob "rumbled" in the spiritual realm all night. "Yea, he had power over the angel, and prevailed: he wept, and made supplication unto him: he found him in Bethel, and there he spake with us ..." (Hosea 12:4).

Pray until something happens. Like his father, Naphtali found liberty through the power of prayer. Prayer changes things. Fights can be won through prayer. Naphtali wrestled to gain his freedom like his father wrestled with an angel. In Genesis 32:24–32, we read of a secret wrestling match. It was not televised—there was no Hulk Hogan or Rock. It was a struggle between Jacob and an unnamed angel, which lasted until Jacob won! Secret victories are sweet though absent of audiences and fanfare. A secret victory is the result of prevailing prayer. Secret victory is when you PUSH—pray until something happens. Naphtali prayed until he was loosed. Do not stop praying until God changes your situation.

Naphtali represents a generation of people who learned how to fight by the spirit. Apostle Paul said, "Fight the good fight of faith, lay hold on eternal life, whereunto thou art also called, and hast professed a good profession before many witnesses" (1 Timothy 6:12). This fight is done in secret, not in public. The process of fighting and "laying hold" of eternal life is a fight to keep the faith. Apostle Paul exhorts the church to act like a soldier (2 Timothy 2:13) and to fight the good fight of faith. Those who overcome the enemy must wrestle their way to victory.

POINTS TO PONDER

The Secret of Naphtali—Secret Wrestling. Naphtali was the sixth son of Jacob and the second son of Bilhah. His name means "wrestling". He represents people who are secretly wrestling with things in their lives, like marriage, a church, a job, their children, or their identity and purpose in life. Everyone is wrestling with something in life. Jacob prophesied that Naphtali and his family would display the characteristics of a deer set free from a trap.

- Everyone struggles with something no matter who they are, but the greatest struggles are those that are kept secret.

- Struggling with something in secret can exert a mysterious power over us if we are not careful.

- Every blade of grass must struggle for sunlight and rain.

- In American culture, people who get trapped are perceived as weak.

- How we react to a struggle can be more important than how we resolve a struggle.

- It can be frightening to feel secretly trapped.

- It has been said that those at war with others are seldom at peace with themselves.

- It is only our spiritual armor and the grace of God that enables us to overcome spiritual warfare.

- Fights won in secret are powerful. Secret victory can be made public by a P.U.S.H—**p**raying **u**ntil **s**omething **h**appens.

- You must hear and understand the Word. You must turn from a self-centered lifestyle to a Christ-centered lifestyle.

- "Rest in the LORD, and wait patiently for him: fret not thyself because of him who prospereth in his way, because of the man who bringeth wicked devices to pass. Cease from anger, and forsake wrath: fret not thyself in any wise to do evil. For evildoers shall be cut off: but those that wait upon the LORD, they shall inherit the earth" (Psalm 37:7–9).

Naphtali secretly wrestled with the "cares of life". He wrestled and resisted until he was set free. Naphtali's younger brother, Gad, was also trapped but overcame until he was set free. Let us take a closer look at Gad and his secret abundance.

CHAPTER 7

THE SECRET OF GAD

SECRET ABUNDANCE

"Gad, a troop shall overcome him: but he shall overcome at the last" (Genesis 49:19).

In this chapter the focus is on secret abundance. Many things can be found in abundance. In these challenging economic times the word "abundance" seems obscure. Why is that? Is it because we only associate abundance with money? *Webster* defines "abundance" as "fullness to overflowing, a great or plentiful amount." So what does abundance mean to you? Once you define "abundance" in your own terms, then the door is open to controlling abundance in your life. How do you go about mastering abundance?

In this chapter, I consider both positive and negative abundance. For example, there are negative and positive numbers in math, and there are also negative and positive charges in the field of electronics. It is the same with abundance—there is a negative abundance and a positive abundance. If you have a great deal of education, such as a Bachelor of Arts, a Master's, and PhD, we may consider you as a person with an abundance of education. If you are unlearned by choice and have fought against education and personal development, then you may be considered as a person who is abundantly ignorant. You can be abundantly sympathetic or abundantly lethargic. You can be abundantly studious or abundantly playful and unfocused. You can be abundantly rich or abundantly poor. The key point is that abundance can be manifested in two forms—negative and positive!

The abundance of a poor widow. Jesus illustrated the principle of secret abundance when he described a poor widow giving an offering at a temple. This illustration of a seemingly negative abundance transformed into a positive abundance. "And he looked up, and saw the rich men casting their gifts into the treasury. And he saw also a certain poor widow casting in thither two mites. And he said, 'Of a truth I say unto you, that this poor widow hath cast in more than they all: For all these have of their abundance cast in unto the offerings of God: but she of her penury hath cast in all the living that she had" (Luke 21:1–4).

The widow was very poor and gave a very small offering. But the secret of her offering was that it was the biggest gift possible. She gave all that she had! The rich men left the temple thinking they had given the biggest gift, but the secret was that it was the poor, old widow who was the richest among them that day. Jesus was so impressed by the woman's giving that he was compelled to speak about her generosity.

Abundance controls your language. An example of negative abundance is a person with a chronic back problem. This person finds no relief and tells others of his or her abundant discomfort, becoming a chronic complainer. Abundance has its own voice. What people say and what people fail to say gives evidence to what is in their heart. Matthew 6:21 says, "For where your treasure is, there will your heart be also."

The abundance of a secret will control your thoughts. Whatever is in abundance will determine the language of the mind. Our conversations and thoughts are fueled by the abundance of secrets. If you knew a thousand secrets about a thousand people, could you keep them all a secret? Would you share just one of them with a dear friend? Withholding or releasing some of those secrets could be therapeutic. There is a liberating effect of letting a secret out.

A wife or mother who has been abused by her husband or a child may find it therapeutic to "get the weight off her shoulders" by telling someone of her pain. People who talk are often helped. Talking about pain is just as important as talking about treatment for the cause of the pain. Do not keep your pain in secret. Empty your bank of pain.

A secret bank account. Everyone has a "bank account" of secret stuff. When that stuff reaches a certain threshold of pain or joy, we open our mouths and declare the abundance to be present. Every person possesses something in great abundance. You may say you have nothing in abundance, but even then your "nothingness" is of great abundance. Abundance determines your destiny. A person's conversation is determined by the abundance in his or her heart. The Bible says in Matthew 12:34, "For out of the abundance of the heart the mouth speaketh." If nothingness is abundant in your heart, then your conversations will reflect nothing of substance. Whatever is in abundance in your heart (faith, love, hatred, fear, worries, peace, doubt, evil, etc.) will proceed out of your mouth. If your mind is full of thoughts about God you will frequently speak about Him.

Speaking often about God. Whatever is in abundance will speak! The prophet Malachi spoke of the people who possessed an abundant reverence for God when he wrote, "Then they that feared the LORD spake often one to another: and the LORD hearkened, and heard it, and a book of remembrance was written before him for them that feared the LORD, and that thought upon his name" (Malachi 3:16). Yes, abundant pain will speak, as will abundant joy. Abundant faith will speak. Abundant fear will speak. Abundant love will speak. Abundant insecurity will speak. Abundant sin and disbelief will speak. Abundant preparation will speak. Abundant visions will speak.

This chapter is about Gad and his secret abundance. We will consider the following aspects of Gad's abundance:

1) Influenced by abundance
2) The secret abundance of Zilpah
3) Dealing with the enemy's secret abundance
4) We shall overcome—"a troop shall overcome him"
5) The sweetness of victory—"but he shall overcome at the last"

Jacob prophesied on his deathbed that Gad would experience great failure but also great victory. Gad's mother, Zilpah, experienced great failures too.

1) Influenced by abundance. There were many people in the Bible influenced by abundance. Let us review a few:

- **Abraham saw secret abundance**. God promised Abraham that his family would be so great and abundant that the number would be compared with the stars of heaven. God wanted Abraham to see and understand the power of abundance. There were too many stars for Abraham to number. He felt overwhelmed but believed in the abundance of God. "And he brought him forth abroad, and said, Look now toward heaven, and tell the stars, if thou be able to number them: and he said unto him, So shall thy seed be. And he believed in the LORD; and he counted it to him for righteousness" (Genesis 15:5).

- **Jacob saw secret abundance**. He saw a multitude or an abundance of angels ascending and descending a ladder from heaven. "And he dreamed, and behold a ladder set up on the earth, and the top of it reached to heaven: and behold the angels of God ascending and descending on it" (Genesis 28:12).

- **Elisha saw secret abundance.** "And he answered, Fear not: for they that be with us are more than they that be with them. And Elisha prayed, and said, LORD, I pray thee, open his eyes, that he may see. And the LORD opened the eyes of the young man; and he saw: and, behold, the mountain was full of horses and chariots of fire round about Elisha" (2 Kings 6:16–17).

- **Jesus demonstrated abundance.** He took two fish and five loaves of bread and was able to feed five thousand people. That is a miracle only Jesus could have performed (Matthew 14:17–21).

- **Paul saw secret abundance in heaven**. He could not talk about it, but he wrote, "And lest I should be exalted above measure through the *abundance of the revelations*, there was given to me a thorn in the flesh, the messenger of Satan to buffet me, lest I should be exalted above measure" (2 Corinthians 12:7).

- **The abundance of His love draws sinners.** "And I, if I be lifted up from the earth, I will draw all men unto me" (John 12:32). God's love is so abundant that it is magnetic. His unmatchable love draws and attracts. The abundant goodness of God causes men's hearts to change. Paul wrote, "Or despisest thou the riches of his goodness and forbearance and longsuffering; not knowing that the goodness of God leadeth thee to repentance" (Romans 2:4). His love and goodness is everlasting and has no limitations. Jeremiah wrote of his everlasting, abundant love, "I have loved thee with an everlasting love, therefore with lovingkindness have I drawn thee" (Jeremiah. 31:3).

2) The secret abundance of Zilpah. Zilpah was a slave. Laban was the slaveowner. Zilpah was a slave of secrecy, silence, and tears.

Zilpah is never quoted in the Bible. Slaves were often not allowed to speak, read or to express themselves. Zilpah lived in her secret little world. Furthermore, Laban gave Zilpah to Leah as a gift to celebrate her marriage to Jacob. The transfer of ownership did not make much difference to Zilpah—she was still a slave. Leah was a proud slave owner. Was Zilpah in good hands, or was she in the hands of an angry, desperate, vindictive woman? Could the transfer from a male slave owner to a female slave owner reduce the probability of abuse? Males abusing women in heterosexual relationships are well-known and documented facts, but how many women in our increasing dominant female culture are secretly abused (verbally, emotionally, or physically) by other women?

As mentioned previously, because Rachel (Jacob's favorite wife) was barren, he consented to impregnate Bilhah, Rachel's handmaid, so that Rachel could have children by proxy. At about this time Leah ceased bearing children, so taking a cue from her younger sister Leah arranged for Jacob to sleep with her handmaid Zilpah.

Rachel adopted two boys through Bilhah (see Figure 7.1). By custom, a son born to a slave woman belonged to the wife of the father. The slave wife had no rights to name her children or to claim ownership of that child. When Leah saw how Rachel adopted two sons, she became angry, jealous and more competitive.

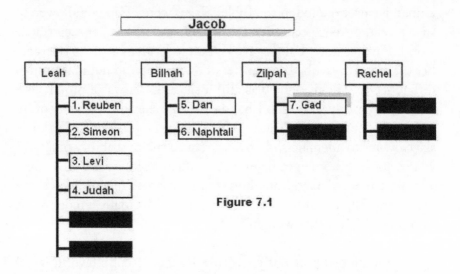

Figure 7.1

Because of her anger, Leah demanded that her slave, Zilpah, sleep with her husband. "Give me a son," Leah demanded, and it happened! Zilpah produced a son for Leah, and Gad became the seventh son of Jacob. Gad was Zilpah's first son, and Zilpah became a pawn between the two fighting sisters. Zilpah carried Gad for nine months, and though she smiled and was pleased when she saw a little baby boy squirming in her arms, she could not respond too happily because it would irritate Leah. The boy belonged to Leah.

Leah named Zilpah's son "Gad," which means, "fortunate, troop, or abundance." "And Leah said, 'A troop cometh': and she called his name Gad" (Genesis 30:11). Again, Zilpah was silent throughout scripture. Does Zilpah have an opinion about her situation? Zilpah means "dripping," "leaking," or "to trickle." Her leaking heart was silent and deeply crying. *Webster's Dictionary* defines trickle as, "to flow in a thin, gentle stream." Zilpah's heart was dripping with emotions of joy and anger. A troop of joy! A troop of pain! Her heart was full. It was difficult for her to contain her emotions because her baby had been taken away from her. Zilpah felt a constant dripping of secret emotions but remained silent. Drip-drop, drip-drop, drip-drop goes the dull sound of water dripping onto the already cold pond.

3) Dealing with the enemy's secret abundance. Jacob blessed Gad, saying on his deathbed, "Gad, a troop shall overcome him: but he shall overcome at the last" (Genesis 49:19). Gad would encounter an abundance of opposition, which would overcome him like a flood. Isaiah said, "When the enemy shall come in like a flood, the Spirit of the LORD shall lift up a standard against him..." (Isaiah 59:19).

Where does the enemy come from? Abba Eban (1915-2002), an Israeli diplomat and politician, gives us a clue to the answer of this question. He states, "You cannot achieve anything without getting in someone's way. You cannot be detached and effective." The enemy can be anyone at any time. Whenever or wherever you are trying to achieve something, no matter how altruistic, there is always someone somewhere who will try to hinder you. The psalmists cried out, "Consider mine enemies; for they are many; and they hate me with cruel hatred" (Psalm 25:19).

The psalmist also complained that his enemies were great in number. Jacob told Gad that he was going to be faced with a great enemy, which would overwhelm him. They would discredit, demote, and attempt to destroy Gad. Jacob could not stop his prophecy. Gad will not be defeated. Jacob said, "Gad shall overcome." Jacob was saying that the enemy would form weapons and use them against Gad, but their weaponry would not prosper. In the words of the prophet Isaiah, Jacob was saying, "No weapon that is formed against thee shall prosper; and every tongue that shall rise against thee in judgment thou shalt condemn. This is the heritage of the servants of the LORD, and their righteousness is of me, saith the LORD" (Isaiah 54:17).

The secret of winning a war is preparing for it in a time of peace. Jesus understood the power of abundance. He preached abundance. He said, "The thief cometh not, but for to steal, and to kill, and to destroy: I am come that they might have life, and that they might have it more abundantly" (John 10:10). Great multitudes were attracted to Jesus and his teachings of abundance. Yet, he pointedly challenged them to consider the power of abundance. He gave several examples in Luke 14:27–32:

- **You must evaluate the abundance of your love before following Christ**. Are you capable of denying yourself? "Then said Jesus unto his disciples, If any man will come after me, let him deny himself, and take up his cross, and follow me." (Matthew 16:24).

- **You must assess your resources (abundance) before engaging in a big project**. Luke said to one such crowd, "For which of you, intending to build a tower, does not sit down first and count the cost, whether he has enough to finish it lest, after he has laid the foundation, and is not able to finish, all who see it begin to mock him, saying, This man began to build and was not able to finish" (Luke 14:28).

- **Preparing for war.** What makes an enemy strong is his abundance or perceived abundance? Jesus said you must determine your level of resources or abundance before engaging in a war. He said, count the cost before you start anything. He said, "What king, going to make war against another king, sitteth not down first, and consulteth whether he be able with ten thousand to meet him that cometh against him with twenty thousand?" (Luke 14:31).

In the above quotations, Jesus used two examples to illustrate the power of abundance. First, he used the example of someone starting an expensive and time-consuming building project, and he noted that no one should begin such an endeavor without first determining that he has enough resources to complete the project. If you miscalculate the level of your abundance, you could fall short and fail. In the second example, he likened abundance to a decision to go to war and initiate a long, drawn-out struggle in which people will face repeated hardship, setbacks, and defeats. Is there a sufficient level of resources to stay committed long enough to win the war?

Pharaoh's confidence in his staff's abundance. Pharaoh was the absolute ruler of Egypt. The book of Exodus described how Pharaoh enslaved the Israelites and refused to let them go. Pharaoh's heart was too hard to respond to God's glory. Pharaoh's hardness of heart was connected to his secret abundance. Pharaoh's advisors told him that their secrets were greater than the secrets of Moses, and the sorcerers and magicians reminded Pharaoh of the secret powers of Egypt, which were in abundance. I believe his counselors and sorcerers declared, "Never give up O Pharaoh, the God of Moses can do some pretty neat tricks, but we have an abundance of tricks in our bags too!"

In the book of Exodus, Pharaoh's sorcerers attempted to match miracle to miracle with God, from turning the waters of the Nile into blood (Exodus 7:22) to causing a plague of frogs (Exodus 8:7). They copied Moses' miracle by turning a rod into a serpent, but their abundance could not compare to the abundance of God. Each time Pharaoh thought of surrendering to Moses' requests, his sorcerers and counselors would advise him of the abundance of secret powers they possessed among the Egyptians.

Hitler's false abundance. The former dictator of Germany, Adolph Hitler, was a psychopath. Hitler killed more than 6 million Jews. He wanted to kill anyone who was not German, or who had any physical or mental problems. Hitler was greatly influence by Charles Darwin and his Theory of Evolution. He believed that the German people possessed a greater abundance of mental and physical abilities. Hitler believed that the German people were the most advanced race of people, and all others were inferior. For Darwin's theory of survival of the fittest to be true, all other inferior species had to die.

His military insanity was also connected to his belief that he possessed weapons of mass destruction. He also believed that he was superior from a military standpoint. He was not afraid of anyone because he was advised (although falsely) of the secret military powers he possessed. Friedrich O. Georg, in his book entitled, *Hitler's Miracle Weapons: Secret Nuclear Weapons of the Third Reich and Their Carrier Systems, Volume 1: Luftwaffe and Kriegsmarine*, suggests that the secret abundance of Hitler's weaponry encouraged him to keep fighting and conquering. Hitler's staff erroneously advised him that they were very close to producing carrier systems for nuclear weapons. Hitler's false aboundance engerized him to keep fighting. Hitler declared, "I will fight until the end!", and trusted in the secret abundance of his arsenal. His German researchers misled Hitler of their progress at producing various weapons of mass destruction, including the atomic bomb. Why should a tyrant quit fighting and conquering when he believes he is more powerful than his enemy?

Your level of abundance will determine your commitment. Our commitment, said Jesus the Messiah, must be total. He said, "And whosoever doth not bear his cross, and come after me, cannot be my disciple" (Luke 14:27). There must be a deliberate commitment to put God above everything else regardless of the cost.

4) We shall overcome—"a troop shall overcome him." Jacob prophesied that Gad would be temporarily defeated. The enemy's abundance would overwhelm and outnumber him. With only a few breaths of life left, Jacob told Gad that he would experience defeat in battle, struggles, and other fights. But we must remember that the battle belongs to the Lord. The prophet Samuel cried, "And all this assembly shall know that the LORD saveth not with sword and spear: for the battle is the Lord's, and he will give you into our hands" (1 Samuel 17:47). The word "overcome" means to conquer. Gad will be temporarily overpowered by his enemy. Gad will lose the battle but he will not lose the war.

5) The sweetness of victory—"but he shall overcome at the last." The key word in this verse is, "but." Have you ever noticed how the word *but* makes a massive difference in how a story ends? God promised Gad victory. Jacob uttered, "...but he shall overcome at the last." Gad's future looked grim, but God promised to be with Gad, says Jacob. In this verse, the word *but* changed everything for Gad. It was an abundant *but*. It was a victorious *but*. It was a triumphant *but*.

Points to Ponder

The Secret of Gad—Secret Abundance. Gad was the seventh son of Jacob. His name means "abundance". His mother's name was Zilpah. Gad represents people who are controlled and influenced by their secret abundance. The abundance of secret thoughts will determine what you say. This means what you treasure the most in your heart will come from your mouth regularly. What comes out of your mouth regularly will determine your destiny. Whatever you possess in surplus (whether good or evil) will control your life and conversation. Jacob prophesied that Gad and his family would display the characteristics of a troop or an army.

- Secret abundance is an effective cause that produces a public effect.

- Anything can be found in abundance.

- There are two types of abundance—negative and positive.

- The richness of a secret will control your thoughts.

- Whatever is in abundance will determine the language of the mind.

- There is a liberating effect of letting a secret out.

- Every person possesses something in great abundance.

- Matthew 12:34 states, "For out of the abundance of the heart the mouth speaketh." Whatever is in abundance in your heart (faith, love, hatred, fear, worry, peace, doubt, evil, etc.) will proceed out of your mouth. Whatever is in abundance will speak!

- "You cannot achieve anything without getting in someone's way. You cannot be detached and effective"— Abba Eban.

- Pharaoh's hardness of heart was connected to his secret abundance.

- Adolf Hitler was not afraid of anyone because he was advised (although falsely) of the secret nuclear power he would soon possess.

- The secret to winning a war is preparing for it in a time of peace.

- Our great example, Jesus Christ, was the greatest "overcomer" in the world.

Gad understood the power of secret abundance. Gad experienced a temporary setback; but his set back was a set-up for a comeback! Can you be happy when faced with setbacks in life? Gad's younger brother, Asher, taught us how to remain happy, even if the happiness is concealed. Let us take a look at the secret happiness of Asher.

CHAPTER 8

The Secret of Asher

Secret Happiness

"Out of Asher his bread shall be fat, and he shall yield royal dainties" (Genesis 49:20).

There are certain times and situations when you must conceal your happiness. Whether winning or losing a contest, happiness can be experienced in just knowing the "fight is over". Some forms of celebration must be suppressed and only expressed in secret. Secret happiness is the process of finding happiness behind the curtains of your pain. It is an awareness that the fight is over and that rewards are on the way. It is hope for tomorrow that awakens and releases that emotion called "happiness." Apostles Paul, Peter, and James gave us examples of secret happiness. They wrote:

"Therefore I take pleasure in infirmities, in reproaches, in necessities, in persecutions, in distresses for Christ's sake: for when I am weak, then am I strong." (2 Corinthians 12:10).

"And they departed from the presence of the council, rejoicing that they were counted worthy to suffer shame for his name." (Acts 5:41).

"My brethren, count it all joy when ye fall into diverse temptations; Knowing this, that the trying of your faith worketh patience." (James 1:2–3).

The above scriptures and similar passages in the Bible help us cope with sufferings. Yes, you can find happiness in the midst of suffering. Apostle Paul wrote that our attitude towards suffering should be quite different from that of unbelievers. He wrote that your happiness is established by your hope, "that ye sorrow not, even as others which have no hope" (1 Thessalonians 4:13). The believer knows that God is in control—the believer knows that God will not allow more temptation and pressure to fall upon him than he or she can bear (1 Corinthians 10:13). He or she also knows that everything is working together for the good because he or she loves God and is called according to his purpose (Romans 8:28). Secret happiness is a silent celebration of knowing that God is going to take suffering and use it for His glory. Dr. Martin Luther King stated in his famous "I have a dream" speech that "unearned suffering is redemptive." In other words, there is a payoff for certain types of suffering.

Secret happiness is the mental condition of being secretly joyous even though you have experienced sacrifice, pain, or loss. The Bible calls for a specific reaction to suffering. This reaction should be practiced in secret and not in the presence of those who would persecute you. Jesus commanded us to express joy when persecuted. Jesus said, "Blessed are ye, when men shall hate you, and when they shall separate you from their company, and shall reproach you, and cast out your name as evil, for the Son of man's sake. Rejoice ye in that day, and leap for joy: for, behold, your reward is great in heaven:

for in the like manner did their fathers unto the prophets." (Luke 6:22–23).

When you secretly rejoice in the midst of an offense, it demonstrates that you are a mature Christian. Jesus said, "Leap for joy" when you are persecuted. You must exercise discretion as to how you rejoice and leap for joy when you are being reproached and persecuted. Such rejoicing for the cause of suffering should be done in secret. Why dance in front of your enemies? You must learn to leap in secret!!

When you practice rejoicing over an offense, it teaches you to stay cool, calm while under stress. The ability to remain secretly happy is powerful. Jesus promised to reward the believer who rejoices in the day of testing and trials; he said, "behold, your reward is great in heaven." (Luke 6:23).

God promised to give you a reward for certain types of sufferings. What kind of reward? It is a secret! But if you practice rejoicing in your tribulation, God will reward you. Let me share three stories of secret happiness.

The secret happiness of my mother's death. On Sunday, May 9, 2004, I stopped by my mother's apartment, in the Homer Phillips Senior Living Center, to deliver a Mother's Day card. I sat on the couch in her small bedroom and watched her breathe her last breath. She died on Mother's Day. I called for her nurses and then I sat there for nearly an hour looking at her lifeless body. As I sat there, I thought no more chemotherapy treatment! No more medicines! No more sleepless nights for her! No more excessive weight loss! No more hospitals! No more disfigured face! Even though I was deeply saddened by the loss of my mother, I was secretly happy that her struggle was over!!!

No one could really understand my sadness or my secret happiness. No longer did I have to conceal my pain when wellwishers inquired of her condition. No more nurses to feed her the liquid diet! I was happy that my mother's suffering had ended—her death was a victory. These types of victories are privately celebrated. It was necessary to conceal my happiness about her death because people would not understand. After sitting for an hour, I began to call relatives to inform them of mom's death and to make arrangements for her funeral, but I was secretly happy that her torment was terminated.

The secret happiness of Mable's divorce. How many wives and husbands have experienced the secret happiness of a divorce? Mable and Roger had been married for nearly ten years. For almost five of those ten years, Roger had been threatening to divorce Mable. Roger would often scream comments like, "We are so incompatible, I do not know why we got married ... you are a terrible wife ... we need a divorce." Mable walked on pins and needles for nearly five years, hoping not to offend Roger and give him cause for divorce. However, in Roger's eyes Mable could never do anything right. He blamed her for everything.

One evening Mable came home and found the house entirely empty. Roger had left a note demanding a divorce. It was painful because Mable felt she had done everything possible to save their marriage. She felt like a failure, but deep in her heart she was secretly happy. It was over! No more walking on pins and needles! No more arguments! No more false accusations and fighting! No more false hopes of saving a dead marriage! Mable never publicly celebrated Roger's departure, yet she was secretly happy that his threats of leaving her and his verbal abuse had come to an end. She could begin a new life without Roger. This was her secret happiness—it was over!

The secret happiness of Al's termination. For two years Al received several letters from his supervisor reprimanding him. His supervisor felt he was extremely disorganized and unproductive. He was placed on probation for poor performance on the job. Al felt the letters of reprimand and probation were unfair. He made every reasonable effort to improve his performance, he thought. His renewed efforts, however, were not sufficient to satisfy his demanding supervisor. Then it happened—Al was terminated and ushered out of the building by security. Al was devastated by the termination, but deep within his heart he was secretly happy. He was free from the harassment of his supervisor, and he could *really* begin to look for a better place of employment. The fight was over!

Have you ever experienced secret happiness after being defeated? Have you ever experienced secret happiness after someone walked out and divorced you? Have you ever experienced secret happiness after being terminated from your job? Have you ever experienced secret happiness once a relative died after a long illness? Have you ever experienced secret happiness after you lost an election or an important contest? Have you ever experienced secret happiness after waiting to hear about a major decision that did not go favorably? There are some struggles, challenges, and defeats that cause us to celebrate because the *battle is over!*

It is true that you are not supposed to be happy when bad things happen to you. You are not supposed to be happy when your mother dies. You are not supposed to be happy when your husband files for divorce. You are not supposed to be happy when you are terminated from your job. You are not supposed to be happy when your child dies after a long period of illness. You are not supposed to be happy when your boyfriend breaks up with you. You are not supposed to be happy when your car breaks down. You are not supposed to be happy when your best friend stops calling. You are not supposed to be happy when you think of the betrayal and the suffering of Jesus. Yet, in all of these examples there is room for happiness. Whether you have won or lost, the happiness is in knowing that the fight is over.

Let us look closer at Jacob's prophecy. Jacob's words show how a Christian should view his or her position in life. While at the portals of death, Jacob turns his attention to his eighth son and speaks words of life. He prophesied, "Out of Asher his bread shall be fat, and he shall yield royal dainties" (Genesis 49:20). These words would catapult Asher with a new impulse of life and vitality.

In this chapter I will consider the following factors concerning Asher's life and his happiness.

1) Zilpah's secret
2) Asher's inner happiness—"Out of Asher"
3) Asher's secret recipes
4) Anna's secret
5) His secret strength

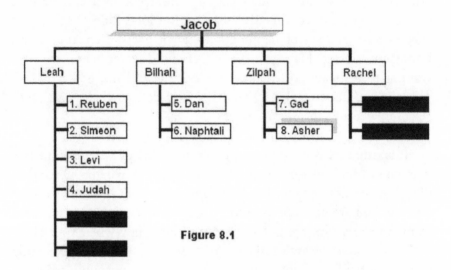

Figure 8.1

1) Zilpah's secret. As shown in Figure 8.1, Zilpah gave birth to two sons (Gad and Asher). I believe she was angry with having to give her sons away, yet I believe that she was proud that she could secretly call them "her sons."

Asher was the eighth son of Jacob. Leah named her second adopted son Asher, which means "Happy am I" (Genesis 30:13). Based on Jacob's prophecy, I believe Asher was happy his entire life. It is remarkable how the names of certain people in the Bible seem to characterize their lives. Asher had a right to be happy. He followed the God of his father, Jacob. The psalmist sang about happiness, to them that followed the God of Jacob, when he wrote, "Happy is he that hath the God of Jacob for his help, whose hope is in the LORD his God" (Psalm 146:5).

God always gives us reasons to be happy. *Webster's Dictionary* defines "happy" as a state of well-being and contentment, good fortune, and prosperity. One reason for Asher's secret happiness was the promise given in Jacob's prophecy. Asher was going to be spiritually rich. Apostle Paul exhorts believers to "rejoice in the Lord always!" (Philippians 4:4).

2) Asher's inner happiness—"Out of Asher." Jacob prophesied that something would come out of Asher". What was in Asher that would come out? "As within, so without." Out of Asher's belly would flow happiness. There are three factors that would contribute to Asher's happiness—they are his insight, his delight, and his uprightness.

His Insight. Asher is happy because he has insight. *Webster's Dictionary* defines insight as "the act of apprehending the inner nature of things or of seeing intuitively." The psalmist declared the power of insight when he wrote, "I have more insight than all my teachers, for I meditate on your statutes" (Psalm 119:99).

Asher gained insight from his personal experiences. He remembered that his mother was a slave. He remembered how God promoted her from a slave to a maid. He remembered how God then promoted her from a maid to a concubine. Then she was promoted from a concubine to one of the mothers of the nation of Israel. The psalmist sings of the secrets of promotion. He declared, "For promotion cometh neither from the east, nor from the west, nor from the south. But God is the judge: he putteth down one, and setteth up another" (Psalm 75:6–7). "Out of Asher" was his insight to God's grace to promote.

His Delight. Jacob declared that Asher has been called to serve royalty. He is happy with his position. With the ability to see intuitively, he found delight in his heritage. Asher delighted in the "heritage of Jacob thy father." Asher's insight of his heritage produced delight. The psalmist declared, "The lines are fallen unto me in pleasant places; yea, I have a goodly heritage" (Psalm 16:6). Again, Isaiah speaks of Jacob's heritage, saying, "Then shalt thou delight thyself in the LORD; and I will cause thee to ride upon the high places of the earth, and feed thee with the heritage of Jacob thy father: for the mouth of the LORD hath spoken it" (Isaiah 58:14).

His uprightness. "Out of Asher" will come uprightness. Uprightness conveys the idea of being morally upright or righteous, not stooping and being anything less than what God has designed you to be. When your conscience is clear you can walk upright. When you are happy you can walk with your head held high. Uprightness means you stand morally straight without any deviations that would cause you to morally 'stoop'. "His seed shall be mighty upon earth: the generation of the upright shall be blessed" (Psalm 112:2).

Asher found delight through obedience. There is only one thing in life that will produce happiness, and that is "total obedience". Jesus was the happiest man who ever lived because he always walked in "perfect obedience". Jesus spoke of this perfect obedience when he delared, "And he that sent me is with me: the Father hath not left me alone; for I do always those things that please him" (John 8:29). Like Jesus, Asher discovered delight in obeying God. The Pslamist declared, "Blessed is the man that walketh not in the counsel of the ungodly, nor standeth in the way of sinners, nor sitteth in the seat of the scornful. But his delight is in the law of the LORD; and in his law doth he meditate day and night" (Psalm 1:1–2).

3) Asher's secret recipes—"his bread shall be fat." While lying on his deathbed, Jacob blessed Asher, saying, "Asher's food will be rich; he will provide delicacies fit for a king" (Genesis 49:20). He would serve kings, and everything that came out of him would be bread for the kingdom. Freshly baked bread is one of life's greatest simple pleasures. Let us consider three aspects of Asher's secret recipes: his preparation, his meditation, and his associations.

His preparation. Notice the order of Jacob's prophecy. First, he speaks of the bread, and then the ability to yield. Preparation reduces fear. Secret preparation allows you to eliminate your public mistakes. Asher was fearless. He baked for the king with boldness. He studied and understood the king's appetites and delights. His secret recipes and preparations increased his confidence and happiness. I believe Asher spent most of his days mixing and kneading loaves of bread by hand. It was strenuous work but great fun!

His meditation. Baking requires patience. Asher was motivated by his secret recipes. As Asher waited beside his oven, he meditated. According to *New Unger's Bible Dictionary*, meditation is defined as, "A private devotional act, consisting of deliberate reflection upon some spiritual truth or mystery, accompanied by mental prayer and by acts of the affection and of the will, especially formation of resolutions as to future conduct." I can see Asher sitting beside a hot oven waiting for the bread to rise. As he waits, he meditates. He meditates on sweet things. He covers his bread with honey. The bread is sweet and fat with flavors. Asher knew how the king expected his pastries!

His associations. "Asher's food will be rich; he will provide delicacies fit for a king" (Genesis 49:20 NIV). Asher was happy because he was associated with the king and the royal household. Asher would yield "royal dainties," which were things that only kings would enjoy eating.

4) Anna's secret. Nearly two thousand years after Jacob's deathbed prophecy, a woman from the tribe of Asher celebrated the redemption of Christ. She is identified in Luke 2:37–38 as a prophetess. She was the daughter of Phanuel of the tribe of Asher. Anna married early in her life, and after seven years of marriage she lost her husband. It was a tremendous loss, but she found solace and peace in daily prayer and fasting. From the time her husband died, she devoted herself to attending upon temple services. She was there continually, maintaining an exemplary example of true piety to all who observed her.

Even though she had no official function at the temple, Anna possessed secret happiness. Due to her great passion for God's presence, she was allowed by the priest to reside in one of the chambers of the women's court. Anna was eighty-four years old when the infant Jesus was presented to the Lord.

We need women like Anna. Despite her misfortune (the premature death of her husband) she found happiness in prayer, fasting, and going to the temple. There are three remarkable factors we must consider about Anna: her vision, her precision, and her decision.

Her vision. Anna was a prophetess with a vision. There are two types of prophets—those who "foretell" and those who "tell forth." A prophet who accurately predicts something that is going to happen - foretells. A prophet who declares what God has already declared – "tells forth." Anna was both. She "foretold" and she "told forth." Anna also had a vision. In Bill Hybels' book *Courageous Leadership*, he defined vision as "a picture of the future that produces passion." I believe Anna had a clear vision of the promised Messiah. The vision caused her to be a woman full of passion.

Her precision. According to Jewish law, a firstborn Hebrew boy must be presented in Jerusalem on two occasions. The first occasion was circumcision on the eighth day (Luke 2:21). The second occasion was the legal requirement of the firstborn son (Numbers 18:15–16) or the dedication service. Anna walked into the room at the precise time Simeon blessed Jesus. When Anna saw the baby Jesus, she recognized that he was the Messiah. God's timing is always perfect. The exact time of Christ's birth was not revealed to Anna, but she knew he was the Messiah at the exact moment she saw his face!

Her decision. Anna made the decision to exalt God in the temple when she recognized Jesus as the Messiah. Because of Anna's intimate knowledge of God's Word, she realized what a momentous occasion it was when she saw the long-awaited Messiah. Anna broke forth in praise for the fulfillment of the divine promises, and at the dedication service she gave a prayer of thanks and made a decision to carry the news of the child to "all who were looking for their redemption in Jerusalem." (Luke 2:38).

5) His secret strength. In Deuteronomy 33:24–25, Moses prophesied regarding the tribe of Asher, saying, "And of Asher he said, Let Asher be blessed with children; let him be acceptable to his brethren, and let him dip his foot in oil. Thy shoes shall be iron and brass; and as thy days, so shall thy strength be"

There are several promises to Asher in this blessing. He would have numerous children, which would make him happy (Psalm 127:6–7). He would be surrounded with plenty. He would be guarded by bars of iron and brass. My focus is on the phrase, "As thy days, so shall thy strength be." Note that it is "days" and not "day." God will give strength for each and every day, but God gives specific strength for specific days. There are three promises we should consider. They are the promise of proportion, power, and presence.

Proportion. God gives strength proportionate to our troubles. "As thy days, so shall thy strength be." A companion Scripture in the New Testament tells us that God regulates our trouble. 1 Corinthians 10:13 says, "There hath no temptation taken you but such as is common to man: but God is faithful, who will not suffer you to be tempted above that ye are able; but will with the temptation also make a way to escape, that ye may be able to bear it."

Power. God is omnipotent. Moses declared that the tribes of Asher would find happiness because of God's omnipotence. He controls every second of every day. God knows what our future will be. We will run out of days before God runs out of power and authority. God promised to love us everyday from everlasting to everlasting. God's love does not change with the day. Isaiah writes, "But they that wait upon the LORD shall renew their strength; they shall mount up with wings as eagles; they shall run, and not be weary; and they shall walk, and not faint" (Isaiah 40:31). Whatever each day brings, God will give us strength enough to meet it.

Presence. According to Moses, Asher also finds joy in God because God will always be there watching and regulating his life. Happiness flows from the Lord's presence. David tells us of secret happiness in the valley of the shadow of death, where he finds happiness because the Lord is present. The psalmist declared "fullness of joy" in God's presence, "Thou wilt shew me the path of life: in thy presence is fullness of joy; at thy right hand there are pleasures for evermore" (Psalm 16:11). The very presence of God will be Asher's strength. The prophet Nehemiah writes, "Neither be ye sorry; for the joy of the LORD is your strength" (Nehemiah 8:10).

POINTS TO PONDER

The Secret of Asher—Secret Happiness. Asher was the eighth son of Jacob. His name means "happy". His mother was also Zilpah. Asher represents people who are secretly happy. The kind of happiness Asher expressed in private is similar to happiness over divorce, secret happiness over the death of a loved one, or secret happiness about being terminated from a job. Jacob prophesied that Asher's family would display the characteristics of one who makes bread and pastries for the king.

- There are certain times and situations when you must conceal your happiness.

- Secret happiness is a silent celebration of knowing that God is going to take suffering and use it for His glory.

- Secret happiness is the mental condition of being secretly joyous even though you have experienced sacrifice, pain, or loss.

- There are some struggles, challenges, and defeats that cause us to celebrate because the *battle is over!*

- When you secretly rejoice in the midst of an offense, it demonstrates that you are a mature Christian.

- God always gives us reasons to be happy.

- There is only one thing in life that will produce happiness, and that is "total obedience".

- Jesus was the happiest man who ever lived because he always walked in "perfect obedience".

- Whatever each day brings, God will give us strength enough to meet it.

Asher understood secret happiness. Asher taught us that when your parent dies, or you lose your job or your spouse divorces you, you can experience secret happiness that is incomprehensible. Faith in God can catapult you to unspeakable happiness. It takes work (study, meditation etc.) to build your faith. Let us turn our attention to the next brother, Issachar, who is known for working in secret.

CHAPTER 9

The Secret of Issachar

Secret Work, Public Reward

"Issachar is a strong ass couching down between two burdens: And he saw that rest was good, and the land that it was pleasant; and bowed his shoulder to bear, and became a servant unto tribute" (Genesis 49:14–16).

There are many organizations that require their employees to maintain the highest level of secrecy. Organizations such as the FBI, CIA, and the Russian KGB all have a history of hiring people who specialize in managing secrets. Because spies work in secret, the public rarely knows when their missions succeed. As President John F. Kennedy said, "Your successes are unheralded and your failures trumpeted." Yes, espionage is big business. Billions of dollars are invested into training and supporting people who must live in secrecy. Other occupations, such as prophets, lawyers modern-day inventors, military strategists, and even criminals, can only be effective by submitting themselves to some degree of secrecy.

From the medical files of a local hospital to the PIN (personal identification number) on a debit card, the management of secrets is crucial for modern, daily survival. The most important inventions, victories, and discoveries have come from people who have worked in secrecy. There are many motives for working in secrecy—whatever the motive, God always knows our motives for keeping things secret.

The X-ray eyes of God. No matter how secret we think our works may be, God sees them, both good and evil. He judges us by our secret motives and actions and weighs our behavior. 1 Samuel 2:3 states, "Talk no more so exceeding proudly; let not arrogancy come out of your mouth: for the LORD is a God of knowledge, and by him actions are weighed." God's eye can be compared to an X-ray machine—he sees through everything and knows our secret works. 2 Chronicles 16:9 says, "For the eyes of the LORD run to and fro throughout the whole earth, to shew himself strong in the behalf of them whose heart is perfect toward him."

The secret of living in the spirit. People who are truly spiritual tend to practice godliness in secret. This does not mean they hide their spiritual identity, for they are not ashamed of being godly. They simply understand that their relationship with God does not require public approval. They are generally not the people who make a lot of noise in church. These are people who diligently study their Bibles in secret, and they privately meditate on the power of God's Word. They memorize scriptures and songs in secret. They repent and confess their faults to God in secret. They live victorious lives.

Candles in Secret. What can conceal the glory of God? Jesus said in Luke 11:33, "No man, when he hath lighted a candle, putteth it in a secret place, neither under a bushel, but on a candlestick, that they which come in may see the light." We must not intentionally conceal our worship, prayer, and giving. Yet, we must live a public and private life of spiritual discipline.

The disciplines of prayer, fasting, stewardship, study, meditating, worship, confessions, and faith are like candles. They cause us to radiate the glory of God. It is impossible to conceal the flames of these candles—they are like a burning bush in a secret place. Spiritual discipline is a work that must be practiced in secret. If they are truly practiced in secret they will be publicly revealed. The effects of practicing our spiritual disciplines in secret can be compared with an atomic bomb exploding in a bungalow home in north St. Louis.

In this chapter we will consider Issachar as a person who is symbolic of people who work in secret. As we analyze the secrets of Issaschar, we will consider the following factors:

1) The secrets of Issachar
2) Issachar—"strong but lazy"
3) Issachar's two burdens
4) Issachar—the wise man of the Old Testament
5) Issachar's slavery

As Jacob lay on his deathbed, he turned toward his ninth son. His body was weak, but his voice was strong. His eyes were blind but his vision was clear. He declared, "Issachar is a strong ass couching down between two burdens: And he saw that rest was good, and the land that it was pleasant; and bowed his shoulder to bear, and became a servant unto tribute" (Genesis 49:14–15).

1) The secrets of Issachar. As shown in Figure 9.1, Issachar was the ninth son of Jacob and the fifth son of Leah. Issachar means "man of reward" or "hired man." The operative words for Issachar are "reward" and "work." Issachar represents men who loved to work in private but afterward receive public recognition for their work.

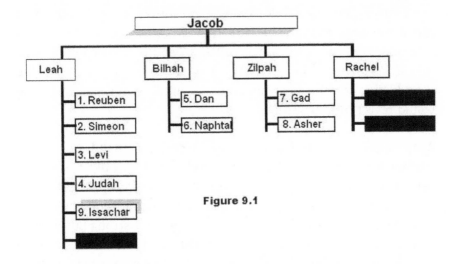

Figure 9.1

She named her son "hire" or "work." Leah believed that God rewarded her with a son because of her kindness to her maid-slave. Leah said, "God hath given me my hire, because I have given my maiden to my husband: and she called his name Issachar" (Genesis 30:18). The name of this son has less to do with Jacob and more to do with Leah's philanthropy.

The prophecy of Jacob. Jacob prophesied that the tribe of Issachar would be like an ass or a donkey. Jacob did not compare Issachar to a horse, an eagle, an ant, or a fish. An ass is not like a horse, it jumps out in front and tries to run ahead of the pack! An ass is impatient and is known to quickly start, but all too often it becomes tired and weary to the point that it just quits and refuses to move. Issachar's family would get a good start but eventually fizzle out.

In Liane Cordes' book entitled, *The Reflecting Pond: Meditations for Self-Discovery* she said, "Continuous effort - not strength or intelligence - is the key to unlocking our potential." Issachar understood the importance of continuous effort.

Characteristics of the donkey. "An ass is a complex creature and capable of many moods. It can be friendly, affectionate, independent, and patient. But when a donkey would rather not do something, it can be the most stubborn creature in the world. The male ass is called a "jackass." A female donkey is called a "jenny." Jacob could foresee that Issachar would be strong but lazy and stubborn as an ass. He would have the ability to work and make intelligent decisions but he would revert to a lazy condition.

2) Issachar—"strong but lazy." Jacob declared that Issachar was "strong as an ass," but Jacob also said that he would find much rest. It was not just rest but "good rest." Some forms of rest injure the soul. Like a donkey, Issachar lacked passion, motivation, and discipline. He became lazy. Issachar was publicly strong but secretly lazy. Issachar was pronounced to be a strong but lazy beast which would become a servant. This prophecy became true. Issachar's tribe did not seize their allotted land from the Canaanites; instead they choose to live wherever they could find a place.

Where does laziness comes from? Laziness comes from an arrogant attitude that one does not need to work for one's food. Issachar "bowed his shoulder to bear." Let us consider six causes of laziness:

- Laziness comes from a lack of vision and passion.

- Laziness comes from a complete lack of motivation.

- Laziness comes from being too comfortable with your lifestyle.

- Laziness comes from deep doubt.

- Laziness comes from poor theology.

- Laziness comes from a lack of discipline.

Colin Powell (former United States Secretary of State) tackled the matter of laziness, he stated, "There are no secrets to success-do not waste time looking for them. Success is the result of perfection, hard work, learning from failure, loyalty to those for whom you work, and persistence."

The burden of balancing the things of life

Figure 9.2

3) Isaachar's two burdens. Figure 9.2 shows two burdens. Jacob saw Issachar as a "strong ass couching down between two burdens." "Couching down" means Issachar was lying down with burdens on his back. The two burdens were Issachar's public life and his secret life. There must be a balance between your public and secret life, because everything cannot be public and everything cannot be secret. Issachar found this balancing act a burden, as both "baggages of life" were heavy.

Trying to balance public and secret things can be difficult. Jesus taught about balance. The religious people of his day had a proclivity for doing everything in public. They gave money in public for the purpose of being seen by others. They prayed and fasted in public for public recognition. They were out of balance. Jesus introduced a new concept about doing spiritual acts in secret. Nothing can be hidden from God.

Three secret works. The Bible describes three secret works that receive public rewards. These are secret works of giving, prayer, and fasting.

The secret of giving. God will reward you publicly. Jesus said if you give in secret "the Father who sees in secret" will reward you publicly. Jesus taught us how to give. He said, "Therefore when thou doest thine alms, do not sound a trumpet before thee, as the hypocrites do in the synagogues and in the streets, that they may have glory of men. Verily I say unto you, they have their reward" (Matthew 6:2).

Issachar represents people who give in secret. Jesus said, "That thine alms may be in secret: and thy Father which seeth in secret himself shall reward thee openly" (Matthew 6:4). The power of giving is in giving in secret. God wants us to give secretly, and he promised to bless us openly or publicly. Jesus condemned those who worked just to be seen by men. Jesus said, "But all their works they do for to be seen of men: they make broad their phylacteries, and enlarge the borders of their garments" (Matthew 23:5). But all their vain efforts would not benefit them.

The secret of prayer. God will reward you publicly for a secret prayer life. Jesus said when you pray, enter into your closet. This means that you must go to a secret place. The Father who sees you praying in secret will reward you publicly. God rewards those who seek after him in prayer. Pray in secret because God hears and answers in secret! Jesus said, "But thou, when thou prayest, enter into thy closet, and when thou hast shut thy door, pray to thy Father which is in secret; and thy Father which seeth in secret shall reward thee openly" (Matthew 6:6). Hebrews states, "But without faith it is impossible to please him: for he that cometh to God must believe that he is, and that he is a rewarder of them that diligently seek him" (Hebrews 11:6). God sees our secret prayers and will reward us for such works. Jesus said those who make long prayers in pretense will be judged for this false work (Mark 12:40).

The secret of fasting. Fast in secret because God hears and answers in secret! "Moreover when ye fast, be not, as the hypocrites, of a sad countenance: for they disfigure their faces, that they may appear unto men to fast. Verily I say unto you, they have their reward. But thou, when thou fastest, anoint thine head, and wash thy face; That thou appear not unto men to fast, but unto thy Father which is in secret: and thy Father, which seeth in secret, shall reward thee openly" (Matthew 6:16–18).

Fast in secret and God will reward you publicly. Much of what the Pharisees gave to themselves was rhetoric, not reality. The appearance of spirituality without the actual sacrifice and rigors of truly praying and fasting was superficial. This was why they were called "whitewashed walls" by Jesus in Matthew 23:27. Fasting in secret does not mean that you never talk about it; it just means that fasting is not a means of gaining the attention of men. Fasting is not designed for some kind of spiritual promotion or as a means of establishing your spiritual superiority over others. The sincere desire to encounter God and the Word through prayer and fasting usually ends with the authentic garment of humility becoming a part of your walk.

Do not stop fasting because you are afraid of pride, and do not over-spiritualize when and how to fast. People who are truly spiritual live much of their lives practicing fasting in secret. They have no need for self-aggrandizement and showmanship. The secret of Issachar is that every secret work will receive its just reward. Whatever a person secretly plants will eventually be revealed. Galatians 6:7 says, "Be not deceived; God is not mocked: for whatsoever a man soweth, that shall he also reap."

4) Issachar—the wise man of the Old Testament. Over hundreds of years, the twelve tribes of Israel developed. Each tribe gained its own reputation. Some tribes were known for worship, as warriors, for their priestly responsibilities, or for their expertise with weapons. But perhaps the most important tribes were those who mastered the secrets of the day. People who decoded and interpreted the secrets of the day were men from the tribe of Issachar (1 Chronicles 12:32). They knew how to apply complex information to action plans. They were known as the ancient strategists. The tribe of Issachar was like the New Testament wise men who located Jesus. They were intelligent. They understood the times and could decipher the secrets of the day.

Spiritual strategies. It is one thing to have access to classified or secret information, and it is quite another to have secret information and know how to apply it to specific situations. The secret of Issachar was that he understood spiritual strategies.

His secret strategies yielded rewards. Issachar was a hard worker and was called a "strong ass" (Genesis 49:14) in reference to his descendants being an agricultural tribe who cultivated their territory with "patient labor." However, Issachar later slacked off and became lazy to the extent that it caused him to become a servant.

The "greatest" secret. It is crucial to know what to do in a time of trouble. David associated himself with men who knew what to do in times of trouble. Before David became King of Israel, he was in exile and running from his father-in-law, King Saul. God sent men to help David, and two hundred of them were from the tribe of Issachar.

The tribe of Issachar possessed the ability to understand the times (secrets) and knew what to do, and this greatly helped the fleeing David. 1 Chronicles 12:32 tell us of Issachar's military ability, saying, "And of the children of Issachar, which were men that had understanding of the times, to know what Israel ought to do; the heads of them were two hundred; and all their brethren were at their commandment."

The gift of strategy. The tribe of Issachar had the gift of strategy. They had sufficient information that allowed them to understand what to do. If you wanted to know what to do in a troubling situation, you had to consult the tribe of Issachar. They had action plans. According to the Targum[91], this meant that Issachar knew how to ascertain the periods of the sun and moon, the intercalation of months, and the dates of solemn feasts, and he could interpret the signs of the times. The tribe of Issachar was known for working in secrecy and creating strategies for warfare.

Who are the "men of Issachar" for our generation? They would be men who have insight to and understanding of the times we are living in. God intended it to be that each generation of believers would think that theirs was the generation chosen to see the Second Coming. The Bible tells us, "No one knows the day or the hour," yet God has set "watchmen on the wall" (Isaiah 62:6) who look for Christ's return and declare that Christ will soon return.

A person's relationship with God starts in secret. The very essence of religion is communion with God, and our communion with God is rooted in secrecy. Our relationship with God starts with the heart. Yet, Jeremiah warned us of the complexities of our hearts. He writes, "The heart is deceitful above all things, and desperately wicked: who can know it?" (Jeremiah 17:9). Our secret, inward relationship with God is invisible to the physical eye. No one can measure the breadth or depth of our relationship with God.

5) Issachar's slavery. Issachar became a slave because he saw that rest was good. Jacob said that Issachar was "as strong as an ass." He was a hard worker. He was the son of a great leader, but he became a slave. He was intelligent but lazy. His hard work led to complacency. He became a slave because he lacked faith ("bowed his shoulders"), he was subject to nature ("he saw the land was pleasant"), he was lazy

---

[9]   *While any translation of the Scriptures may in Hebrew be called a Targum, the word is used especially for a translation of a book of the Hebrew Bible into Aramaic.*

("he saw that rest was good"), and he lost battles with his enemies and became discouraged ("couching down"). He was unwilling to develop a balanced life. He was in conflict "between two burdens". He could not pay his debts, so he "became a servant."

POINTS TO PONDER

The Secret of Issachar—Secret Work, Public Reward. Issachar was the ninth son of Jacob and the fifth son of Leah. His name means, "reward for labor". Issachar represents people whose secret works are made public. Jesus said secret prayer, secret fasting, and secret giving are secret labors that cannot be hidden. Jacob prophesied that Issachar's family would display the characteristics of a donkey.

- There are many organizations that require their employees to maintain the highest level of secrecy.

- The very essence of religion is communion with God, and our communion with God is rooted in secrecy.

- Billions of dollars are invested into training and supporting people who must live in secrecy.

- The most important inventions, victories, and discoveries have come from people who have worked in secrecy.

- 1 Chronicles 12:32 tells us of Issachar's military ability when it says he knew what to do in troubled times.

- When you consistently and relentlessly praise and worship God in secret, it changes your personality.

- We should never become discouraged when men fail to reward us for our works. God knows our works and will reward us.

- God knows every detail of our past, present, and future. He maintains a panoramic view of our lives. His is all-comprehensive.

Issachar understood the importance of doing things in a secret place. However Zebulun, his younger brother, understood it is not how hard you work in secret that determines your payout, it is where you work. Let us look at Zebulun as we consider the power of a secret place.

CHAPTER 10

THE SECRET OF ZEBULUN

SECRET PLACES

"Zebulun shall dwell at the haven of the sea; and he shall be for an haven of ships; and his border shall be unto Zidon" (Genesis 49:13).

This chapter is about finding a secret place. Finding a secret place means finding a place of silence and solitude. Everyone needs a place for self-discovery. And not just any place—only a secret, silent place creates an atmosphere for a renewed and transformed mind (Romans 12:1-2). God teaches you to trust him in secret places, for faith is built in dark secret places. The psalmist declared, "He made darkness his secret place; his pavilion round about him were dark waters and thick clouds of the skies" (Psalm 18:11). A secret place is where your soul communes with God.

The Psalmist declared that power and the presence of God abides in secrecy, saying, "He that dwelleth in the secret place of the most High shall abide under the shadow of the Almighty" (Psalm 91:1). The Psalmist recognized that dwelling in "the secret place" with God created a sense of security and rest. The greatest secret of this generation is that we sit in heavenly places in Christ Jesus (Ephesians 6:2).

Where is this heavenly place? Are we sitting there now? Heaven is a real place, but it is a secret place. The same is true for hell. Heaven and hell are the world's two greatest secrets. Jesus spoke more about hell than any other prophet. He did not want anyone to go there. However, one day heaven and hell will no longer be a secret. Until heaven and hell are totally revealed, we need a secret place.

God knows that we all need a secret dwelling place. God has provided every generation with a "dwelling place." The Psalmist declared, "LORD, thou hast been our dwelling place in all generations." (Psalm 90:1). Yes, we can live in God, we can "dwell" in Him.

At times you may feel like God has abandoned you, but allow me to comfort you with the words of Jesus. He assured his disciples and followers that he has prepared a place for us. He guaranteed believers a location. God promised mansions that we can claim as ours. Jesus said: "Let not your heart be troubled; you believe in God, believe also in me. In my father's house are many mansions; if it were not so, I would have told you. I go to prepare a place for you. And if I go and prepare a place for you, I will come again and receive you to myself; that where I am, there you may be also. And where I go you know, and the way you know" (John 14:1–4). Jesus promised eternal communion with the Father.

There is no communion with God without being in his presence. God is a god of communion. Moses found a secret place of communion which God called "holy ground" (Exodus 3:5). You must stand on holy ground to commune with God. Holy ground is where God speaks. It is a place where you enter into private devotion and conversation with God. Everybody needs a secret place. Everybody needs holy ground.

The Bible provides many examples of men and women who escaped to holy ground. The methods of escaping to this secret place have been a word from God, prayer, worship, dreaming, visions, and meditating. The revelations of God's promises and covenants are found in the secret place. "The secret of the Lord is with them that fear Him" (Psalm 25:14). God can satisfy your longings and deepest desires in the secret place.

A rhema word. Maybe your heart yearns to know the Father in an intimate way. Perhaps you desire revelations and a rhema word from God. The rhema Word is an individual word for a single believer as God speaks particularly through a prophetic ministry, through His Word or through any given individual. To receive a rhema word, you must seek quietness and anonymity in his presence. Psalm 16:11 says, "In thy presence is fullness of joy." A secret place with God is a place of joy and treasures.

Treasures of darkness. God declared that riches are found in secret places. He said, "And I will give thee the treasures of darkness, and hidden riches of secret places, that thou mayest know that I, the LORD, which call thee by thy name, am the God of Israel" (Isaiah 45:3). Everyone needs a place to which they can retreat from the pressures of life and discover the treasures of darkness.

There are different types of secret places. Some secret places are healthy and others are toxic. Apostle Paul declared that treasures that God has prepared for us remain a secret. He wrote, "But as it is written, Eye hath not seen, nor ear heard, neither have entered into the heart of man, the things which God hath prepared for them that love him (1 Corinthians 2:9).

Location, location, location. The slogan of the retail world is, "location, location, location." If you want to be successful in retail you must be in the right place. Location factors for retailers are accessibility, convenience, and the available customer base. However, spouses understand the importance of location. For example, husbands and wives have built their own secret places to find solace. They have built workshops in their basement or work late hours on their jobs in search of that secret place. King Solomon understood the importance of a secret place when he wrote, "It is better to dwell in the corner of the housetop, than with a brawling woman and in a wide house" (Proverbs 25:1). Some people have found hiding places in life by being preoccupied with raising their children. Other people have escaped to their secret places by hiding in their hobbies, video games, TV programs, and the like. Are you looking for a hiding place or a getaway?

How prisoners survived. Prisoners of war have told stories of how they survived deplorable prison camps—they found secret places. They escaped the mental chains of oppression while still in bondage. Jews of the Holocaust and other untold heroes were able to survive death camps by escaping to a secret place within the camp or the secret vicissitudes of their minds. In spite of their bondage, they saw things differently. Like traveling through a time machine, they mentally visited other places outside of their present suffering and confinement. They dreamed. They envisioned themselves liberated. They found secret hiding places within themselves and escaped mental suffering. Keep in mind that a secret place is not necessarily a physical location.

The importance of a secret place. Every time Jesus went to his secret place to pray, it thundered in hell. Demons trembled. Jesus felt it necessary to escape to a secret place. Early in Mark's gospel we find Jesus' need to go to a secret place after healing, casting out demons, preaching, and teaching. Mark 1:35–39 says, "Very early in the morning, while it was still dark, Jesus got up, left the house and went off to a solitary place, where he prayed." (Jesus knew how important it was to escape to a secret place. He did not allow the hurry and the busyness that was thrust upon him by his followers to control him. He knew the benefits of separating himself for even just a moment. In the words of an old preacher named Vance Havner, "Jesus knew how to come apart before he came apart."

The secret places of Jesus. At the beginning of Jesus' ministry, he was led to the desert to spend forty days in secrecy (Matthew 4:1–11). Before he chose the twelve disciples, he slipped away to a secret place in the desert hill (Luke 6:12). When he received news of John the Baptist's death, he "withdrew from there in a boat to a lonely place apart" (Matthew 14:13). After a wonderful display of God's power in the feeding of the five thousand, Jesus needed a secret place. He "went up into the hills by himself" (Matthew 14:23). The Scripture says, "And in the morning, rising up a great while before day, he [Jesus] went out, and departed into a solitary place, and there prayed" (Mark 1:35). Following the healing of a leper, Jesus "withdrew to the wilderness and prayed" (Luke 5:16). As he prepared for his death, Jesus needed to find a secret place in the garden of Gethsemane (Matthew 26:36–46) in order to hear the divine voice of God.

Everyone needs a secret, solitary place. A secret place is powerful thing because "the voice of silence" molds our character and ultimately our destiny. In the secret place God impregnates our heart with the seed of faith.

People in the Bible who found secret places. There are many characters in the Bible who sought for and found secret places. From the very beginning of time humans have desired secrecy. Below is a list of a few characters in the Bible who sought and found a secret place. The list is not exhaustive, but it gives you an idea of the need or desire for secret places.

- **A secret place in Eden.** Adam and Eve were the first to seek a secret place in paradise. They wanted to escape their shame. "And they heard the voice of the LORD God walking in the garden in the cool of the day: and Adam and his wife hid themselves from the presence of the LORD God amongst the trees of the garden (Genesis 3:8).

- **The High Priest**. He entered into the secret place, or the Holy of Holies, each year for the atonement of the people (Exodus 30:10).

- **King David**. He sought a secret place to escape the wrath of his father-in-law, King Saul (1 Samuel 23).

- **An army found a hiding place**. "When the men of Israel saw that they were in a strait (for the people were stressed), then the people did hide themselves in caves, and in thickets, and in rocks, and in high places, and in pits" (1 Samuel 13:13).

- **Fifty prophets found a hiding place**. During Elijah's absence, Ahab's wife, Jezebel, ordered that all prophets of God be executed. Obadiah, one of the king's ministers, hid fifty of them in a cave, where he met Elijah on his way back to Ahab's court (1King 18:4)

- **Jesus hid in Egypt**. Mary and Joseph hid in Egypt for about three and half years, having fled from wicked Herod (Matthew 2:13–15).

- **Apostle Paul**. He found a secret place and hid for three years after his experience on the road to Damascus (Galatians 1:18).

In our secret places, there is an inclination to think about secret things, to talk about secret things, and to do secret things. Secret places truly are powerful things in our lives. You see it is the secret places in our lives that really mold our thinking and shape our emotions. Secret places stimulate us. In this chapter we will consider secrets of Zebulun. Zebulun represents secret places. The following topics will be discussed:

1. Leah's secret
2. Zebulun's secret
3. The secret position of Zebulun
4. The secrets of the sea

1) Leah's secret. Figure 10.1 shows that Zebulun was Leah's sixth and last son and the tenth son of Jacob. Leah hoped that Jacob would come "to dwell" with her because of the birth of her sixth son. The stress resulting from Jacob's love towards Rachel caused Leah to name her son Zebulun, which in Hebrew means "habitation" or "to dwell." "And Leah said, God hath endued me with a good dowry; now will my husband dwell with me, because I have born him six sons: and she called his name Zebulun" (Genesis 30:20).

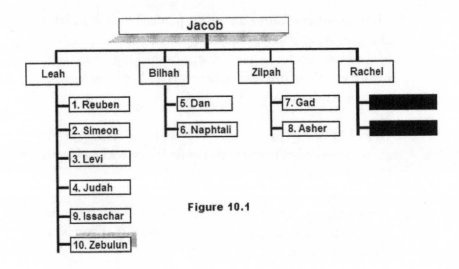

Figure 10.1

Leah's deepest desire was that her husband's cold heart would grow warm towards her. Leah felt that giving Jacob many sons would change his feelings—her sons were gifts or even bribes in exchange for love. She hoped that her gifts would convert his anger to love. "A gift in secret pacifieth anger: and a reward in the bosom strong wrath" (Proverbs 21:14). Jacob's heart, however, remained with Rachel. Once again, the birth of her sixth son did not improve her relationship with Jacob.

A prisoner of love. Leah's deepest secret was that she was a prisoner of love. A prisoner of love is unhappier than a prisoner of war. A prisoner of love cannot break free. A prisoner of love cannot sing a love song. A prisoner of love cannot find vital emotional support to ease their emptiness. A prisoner of love cannot be considered for parole. A prisoner of love cannot appeal to the warden. Yes, Leah's love imprisoned her to a man who did not love her.

2) Zebulun's secret. As Jacob lay on his deathbed, he turned to Zebulun and uttered twenty-five words that revealed two powerful prophecies that would come to pass in the following five hundred years: "Zebulun shall dwell at the haven of the sea; and he shall be for an haven of ships; and his border shall be unto Zidon" (Genesis 49:13).

Jacob's prophecy concerning Zebulun did not consist of prophets, priests, or kings. Neither did it consist of wisdom, riches, or power. There were no heroes or notable characters from the linage of Zebulun. The power of Jacob's prophecy for Zebulun lay in "location." Remember—location, location, location. The Zebulunites left no great legacy, and the only thing that we can say concerning Zebulun is that God gave him a secret place and purpose at the sea.

Secret places and purposes truly are powerful things in our lives. Secret places are the environments that really mold our personality and shape our future. Everyone needs a place where they can breathe freely and hear nothing but the quiet and gentle voice of God. Throughout the ages people have found secret places to escape the pressures of life. Some have been successful, but many have been unsuccessful. Jacob's prophecy promised Zebulun a "position and purpose" by the sea.

Position and Purpose. Jacob stated that Zebulun would "dwell at the haven of the sea," which meant Zebulun would have a position and would live by the sea. Jacob also stated that Zebulun would "be an haven for ships," which meant Zebulun would have a purpose. Zebulun would provide a place of refuge and security. This prophecy was twofold because it assured Zebulun that he would have access to the sea and would be a sanctuary or shelter for ships. This was a strange prophecy because Jews had little experience with the sea, as navigation was not practiced by the Israelites. Noah's Ark was the only ship that they were familiar with (Genesis 6–9). The Israelites were an agricultural nation, and yet Jacob prophesied that Zebulun would "dwell at the sea" and not on a farm. Jacob's prophecy dealt with the whereabouts of Zebulun. Zebulun was going to dwell by the sea and learn all the secrets of the sea.

3) The secret position of Zebulun.

Land-locked or not? Figure 10.2 shows where the twelve tribes settled after they crossed the Jordan River into Canaan Land. The tribe of Zebulun was land-locked by four other tribes—Asher, Naphtali, Issachar, and Manasseh. How could Zebulun be a haven for ships when there was no water around him?

The Twelve Tribes in Canaan

ZEBULUN IS NOT BY THE SEA...IT IS LAND LOCKED

"Zebulun shall dwell at the haven of the sea; and he shall be for an haven of ships: and his border shall be unto Zidon." Gen 49:13

Figure 10.2

As shown above in Figure 10.2, Josephus the renowned Jewish historian helped to answer this question. Josephus says that Zebulun, in fact, extended from the Sea of Galilee to the Mediterranean Sea. When Joshua led Israel into Canaan, the tribes did not conquer all of the land, as God commanded them to (Judges 1:28–36). As shown in Figure 10.2, Joshua assigned the tribe of Zebulun to a portion of land where it would be landlocked. However, as shown in Figure 10.3, while on his deathbed, Jacob could foresee that Zebulun would not be land-locked by four other tribes and that the borders would change over the years.

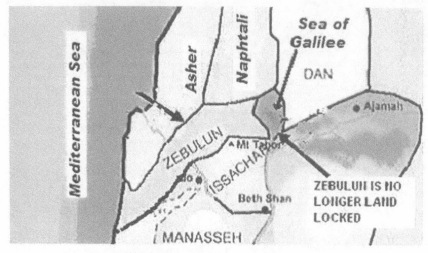

Figure 10.3

Figure 10.3 shows how God enlarged the territory of Zebulun (1 Chronicles 4:10), expanding its boundaries all the way to the Sea of Galilee and Mediterranean Sea. Therefore the prophecy is true. Zebulun "shall dwell at the haven of the sea" and "he shall be a haven of ships." Location, location, location! God appointed where Zebulun would live—"at the haven of the sea"—and God appointed that Zebulun would be "a haven of ships." God determines *where* you shall go and *who* you shall be in life.

Nazareth is in Zebulon! In the New Testament, Zebulun is referred to as "location" and spelled, "Zebulon." Zebulun's tribe settled in the forested hills of southern Galilee around Nazareth, which was later the homeland of Jesus (Matthew 4:12–14). Mary and Joseph fled from Nazareth to a secret place in Egypt, where they hid to escape the wicked plans of King Herod. The family remained there for about three and a half years, and when Herod died they returned home to Nazareth. They actually returned to Zebulon because Nazareth is in Zebulon! Did you know that Jesus ministered more in Zebulon than in any other place? Out of the three and a half years that Jesus ministered on earth, two and a half of them were in Galilee, and

Galilee is in Zebulon! It has been stated that he ministered to *all* of the cities of Galilee during his days on earth.

4) The secrets of the sea. Zebulun would "dwell at the sea" and learn things about the sea. Zebulun would overcome the water (ocean and sea) which covers about 71 percent of the earth's surface. The temperature of most ocean water is about 39 degrees Fahrenheit (4 degrees Celsius), which is just a few degrees above freezing! Zebulun would overcome the freezing waters and master the secrets of the sea. The sea represents people living in darkness (Isaiah 57:20).

In the land of Zebulon there would be a man named Jesus who would preach mercy and giving light in darkness. Sin would be uncovered in this place called Zebulon. If sin is to be defeated it must be exposed. It cannot remain a secret. The Book of Proverbs say you must confess it and forsake it. "He that covereth his sins shall not prosper: but whoso confesseth and forsaketh them shall have mercy" (Proverbs 28:13).

The secret purpose of Zebulun. The wisest man to ever live before Jesus, King Solomon, was mesmerized by the secrets of a ship at sea. King Solomon speaks of his wonder in the book of Proverbs, "There be three things which are too wonderful for me, yea, four which I know not: The way of an eagle in the air; the way of a serpent upon a rock; the way of a ship in the midst of the sea; and the way of a man with a maid" (Proverb 30:18–19). The ship at the sea, which fascinated King Solomon, has become a place of residency for Zebulun. Zebulun would become acquainted with the operations and the secrets of the ship's missions.

Jacob prophesied that Zebulun would be "an haven for ships." The word "haven" means a place of safety, and the word "heaven" is derived from haven. Zebulun would be a "Haven of the Sea; a Haven of Ships." There is a difference between a port and a haven. A port is where ships go in and out to exchange cargo. A haven is where ships rest in peace in times of storm and trouble. In the land of Zebulun, no sound was sweeter than the rattling of chains as shipmen let down their anchor. Jesus is a lighthouse in Zebulun that draws men to truth. "Then they cry unto the LORD in their trouble, and he bringeth them out of their distresses. He maketh the storm a calm, so that the waves thereof are still. Then are they glad because they be quiet; so he bringeth them unto their desired haven" (Psalm 107:28–30).

Jacob knew that Zebulun would be "as a hiding place from the wind." He foresaw that the gospel would first be preached in Zebulon, and the words that Jesus preached would become a hiding place from the effects of sin. Zebulon would become a place of safety (a haven) because of the preaching of the truth there. Jacob knew that was Zebulun's purpose. He would be blessed because of his position. Isaiah says, "And a man shall be as an hiding place from the wind, and a covert from the tempest; as rivers of water in a dry place, as the shadow of a great rock in a weary land" (Isaiah 32:2).

Secrets of the entrepreneur. Every successful business has an inventory of secrets. It must have a process or formula that is kept secret because company secrets keep companies competitive. Jacob knew that Zebulun would operate a lucrative business. He would learn the secrets of the sea. "They that go down to the sea in ships, that do business in great waters" (Psalm 107:23). Zebulun would do business on the sea and at the borders of the sea. If he had no business, there would be no need to venture into the sea. His business would be preaching the gospel and his ministry would be great.

POINTS TO PONDER

The Secret of Zebulun—Secret Places. Zebulun was the tenth son of Jacob. His name means "dwelling". Leah was his mother. Zebulun represents people who understand the importance of dwelling in a secret place—everybody needs one. Jacob prophesied that Zebulun and his family would display the characteristics of a haven or refuge for ships from the sea.

- Everyone needs a private place for his or her needs to be met. People cannot do a good job or relate to others unless their own needs are met.

- Secret places are powerful things because "the voice of silence" molds our character and ultimately our destiny. Turn off the TV, radio, computer, and ipod and listen to God.

- It was necessary for Jesus to find a secret place. He needed to get away from the hustle and bustle of life. In the words of an old preacher, Vance Havner, Jesus knew how to "come apart before he came apart." You must find time alone.

- Some of the happiest people in the world discovered their happiness in the secret place of the most high (Psalm 91:1).

- There is no communion without communication. God wants to meet us in the secret place.

- God reveals himself in secret places.

- A secret place is not necessarily a physical, tangible place—it can be a non-physical location.

- Secret places tend to stimulate you. It can stimulate you to do good or evil.

- God determines *where* we shall go and *who* we shall be in life.

Zebulun knew the importance of finding a secret place. However, his brother Joseph understood that dreaming is not restricted to a place. From a prison to a palace, Joseph learned about the power of a dream. Let us see how the secret dreams of Joseph became a journey of faith into unknown territory.

CHAPTER 11

THE SECRET OF JOSEPH

SECRET DREAMS

"Joseph is a fruitful bough, even a fruitful bough by a well; whose branches run over the wall ..." (Genesis 49:22).

Dreams are powerful. Dreaming is one method by which God communicates with us (Joel 2:28). Dreams were used quite frequently in the Old Testament, but in the New Testament God's primary way of speaking to us is through preaching and the Holy Spirit. If there is conflict between a dream and the Scripture, then the Scripture must take precedent. If your dream is consistent with the messages in the

Bible, there is a good chance that God is speaking to you. Never put a dream before a Scripture.

In the Bible, stories of dreams and their interpretations abound. The power of a dream cannot be released until you wake up, plan, and connect it with action. Most dreams should be kept secret. Joseph's brothers became envious and malicious toward him when he prematurely shared his dreams with them (Genesis 37:5). Perhaps you are dreaming of building a new home, starting a new business, starting a new weight-loss program, writing a book, or taking piano lessons at age sixty. Whatever your dream, you simply cannot tell everyone. Do not broadcast your dreams. Let others find out about your dream through other means. Let them hear it "through the grapevine" that your new home is under construction. Sharing your dreams with the wrong folks can be unproductive and sometimes even counterproductive. Some people are intimidated when they hear about your grandiose dreams. They may even feel envious because they lack such a dream. And a dream is delicate. It can be killed by a sneer or a yawn, it can be terribly distorted by an untimely joke, or it can be crushed by a frown. Certain dreams should be limited to a trusted few and kept secret at the infancy stage.

If you share your dreams with too many folks, you may experience a "dream miscarriage." It is possible to lose the energy and synergy of your dream, so you must be cautious and examine your motive for sharing your secret dreams. When the dream is birthed and becomes reality, it will not be necessary to keep it a secret any longer—it will then be time to testify and give God the glory for what he has performed.

We often prematurely share our dreams because we do not fully understand them. We hope that someone else will give us insight or interpretation. Dreams are secret thoughts until they are expressed. Sometimes it is difficult to separate a dream from reality. Sometime we need a reality check. The difference between a dream and reality is work; that is what makes dreams become real. Dreams can lead people to a great deal of self-discovery. You need to have dreams.

Everything starts with a dream. You can kill men and cripple nations, but you cannot destroy a God-given dream. It is safe to argue that Dr. Martin Luther King Jr. did not prematurely share his dream. His dream consisted of brotherhood and equity for all Americans. He said that his dream was inspired by God not the U.S. Constitution. What is a dream?

"I have a dream." *Webster's Dictionary* defines dream as, "a state of mind in which images, thoughts, and impressions pass through the mind of a person who is sleeping." Dreams remove us from a state of reality. They elevate our thinking to seeing, believing, and doing the impossible. On August 28, 1963, Dr. Martin Luther King, Jr., delivered a speech entitled, "I have a dream". In this speech, King addressed a massive group of civil rights marchers gathered around the Lincoln Memorial in Washington, DC. The march on Washington was for jobs and freedom, and it brought together the nation's most prominent civil rights leaders, along with tens of thousands of marchers, to press the United States government for equality.

Let us turn our attention to a few biblical characters and the stories of their dreams and their interpretations. God keeps giving you dreams to fuel your faith. Below are examples of various characters whose dreams impacted their destiny. This list is not exhaustive, but it illustrates the power of secret dreams.

Jacob dreamed of angels ascending and descending from heaven on a ladder. "And he dreamed, and behold a ladder set up on the earth, and the top of it reached to heaven: and behold the angels of God ascending and descending on it" (Genesis 28:12).

Joseph dreamed of promotion. Joseph dreamed that his brothers would one day bow down before him (Genesis 37:5–11).

Joseph interpreted dreams. The butler and the baker were servants of the pharaoh who were bound in the prison (Genesis 40:5–8). They both had dreams while in prison, and Joseph interpreted their dreams and said that the butler was to be restored to the Pharaoh's favor in three days; the baker was to be hanged in three days. Three days passed. The butler was restored; the baker was hung.

Pharaoh dreamed of a feast and a famine. Pharaoh's dream of the seven lean kine (cattle) devouring the seven fat kine was interpreted by Joseph as seven years of plenty followed by seven years of famine (Genesis 41:1–15). The interpretation of this dream was a turning point in Joseph's life.

A Midianite dreamed of being defeated by Gideon's army. "And when Gideon was come, behold, there was a man that told a dream unto his fellow, and said, Behold, I dreamed a dream, and, lo, a cake of barley bread tumbled into the host of Midian, and came unto a tent, and smote it that it fell, and overturned it, that the tent lay along" (Judges 7:13). The interpretation of this dream was a turning point in defeating the Midianites.

Daniel interpreted Nebuchadnezzar's dream. "And in the second year of the reign of Nebuchadnezzar Nebuchadnezzar dreamed dreams, wherewith his spirit was troubled, and his sleep brake from him. And the king said unto them, I have dreamed a dream, and my spirit was troubled to know the dream" (Daniel 2:1–2). Daniel's interpretation of Nebuchadnezzar's dream opened the door to promotion and influence.

Daniel interpreted Belshazzar's dream. "In the first year of Belshazzar king of Babylon Daniel had a dream and visions of his head upon his bed: then he wrote the dream, and told the sum of the matters" (Daniel 7:1). Daniel saw the empires that were to come. God gave Daniel great insight into the future events that are still unfolding today.

Solomon dreamed. "In Gibeon the LORD appeared to Solomon in a dream by night: and God said, Ask what I shall give thee" (1 Kings 3:5).

An angel spoke to Joseph in a dream. "But while he thought on these things, behold, the angel of the Lord appeared unto him in a dream, saying, Joseph, thou son of David, fear not to take unto thee Mary thy wife: for that which is conceived in her is of the Holy Ghost" (Matthew 1:20).

Herod's wife dreamed of Jesus' innocence. "When he was set down on the judgment seat, his wife sent unto him, saying, Have thou nothing to do with that just man: for I have suffered many things this day in a dream because of him" (Matthew 27:19).

When faced with sickness and physical challenges, a dream can give you the energy to fight. The prophet Joel spoke of the importance of a dream. Joel prophesied that the church would have dreams and visions, saying, "And it shall come to pass afterward, that I will pour out my spirit upon all flesh; and your sons and your daughters shall prophesy, your old men shall dream dreams, your young men shall see visions: And also upon the servants and upon the handmaids in those days will I pour out my spirit" (Joel 2:28–29).

As Jacob lay on his deathbed he turned to Joseph and uttered a powerful prophecy. The word "blessing" was used five times in this prophetic pronouncement. Jacob was blind and old, and he anticipated that he would soon die. Through his faith, Jacob saw a picture of the future. His twelve sons surround his bed and he uttered a prophetic word to Joseph: "Joseph is a fruitful bough, even a fruitful bough by a well; whose branches run over the wall: The archers have sorely grieved him, and shot at him, and hated him: But his bow abode in strength, and the arms of his hands were made strong by the hands of the mighty God of Jacob; (from thence is the shepherd, the stone of Israel:) Even by the God of thy father, who shall help thee; and by the Almighty, who shall bless thee with blessings of heaven above, blessings of the deep that lieth under, blessings of the breasts, and of the womb: The blessings of thy father have prevailed above the blessings of my progenitors unto the utmost bound of the everlasting hills: they shall be on the head of Joseph, and on the crown of the head of him that was separate from his brethren" (Genesis 49:22–26).

Let us now consider the secret dreams that affected Joseph's life. His mother dreamed of having many children. His father dreamed that one day he would enter into the "promise land." Joseph's enemies dreamed of killing him and Joseph dreamed of promotion.

1) A mother's secret dream
2) Dreaming beyond the walls
3) The secret dreams of his enemies
4) The secrets of Joseph's victory
5) The secrets of a threefold blessing

1) A mother's secret dream. For many years Rachel dreamed of having a baby, and finally she gave birth to a little boy. Consider the faith of Rachel. After enduring a long period of barrenness, God opened her womb and gave her a son. She then declared that God was going to do it again! She declared that God was going to keep adding children to her life, and she claimed that she would be fruitful.

If we closely examine the words of Rachel, it seems clear that her secret dream was to have as many sons as Leah. She declared that God had "taken away my reproach." Rachel seemed to believe that God was no longer angry with her and was ready to bless her with a large family. "And God remembered Rachel, and God hearkened to her, and opened her womb. And she conceived, and bare a son; and said, God hath taken away my reproach: And she called his name Joseph; and said, The Lord shall add me another son" (Genesis 30:22–24).

As shown in Figure 11.1, Joseph was the eleventh son of Jacob and the first son of Rachel. The story of Joseph starts in a pit and ends in a palace—from rags to riches. Joseph never lost sight of his

God and his dreams. The name "Joseph" means, "addition," "exceed," "increase," and "conceive again". Joseph was a man who had many dreams. Dreams can encourage you through difficult times. When your family and friends turn against you, a dream can keep your pain from turning into bitterness. When people persecute and lie to you without cause, a dream can comfort you.

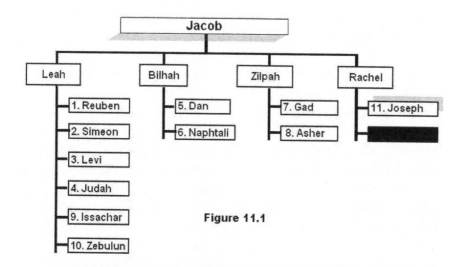

Figure 11.1

Who would have guessed that Joseph would be the savior of his family? As a young boy, Joseph did not fully understand the meaning of his dreams, but they all had meaning. A dream without interpretation is meaningless. The secret power of Joseph was his God. God enabled Joseph to nourish and comfort his family, and God allowed him to save Egypt from the famine.

Joseph spent years in prison, and while there he dreamed. He was the most unlikely candidate to become the prime minister of Egypt. Yet within a few years, he was promoted from the rank of an enslaved, Hebrew prisoner (on an attempted rape charge) to second-in-command to the most powerful man on earth at the time.

2) Dreaming beyond the walls. "Joseph is a fruitful bough, even a fruitful bough by a well; whose branches run over the wall" (Genesis

49:22). There are three attributes to consider about Joseph—his fruitfulness, his well, and his wall.

Joseph is fruitful in a dysfunctional family. He is fruitful in prison. He is fruitful in Egypt. Joseph meditates on the things he knows about God. His heart is fixed on God (Psalm 57:7). His testimony is that "Princes have persecuted me without a cause; but my heart standeth in awe of thy word" (Psalm 119:161). Because of his incorruptible seed, Joseph stands strong.

The secret of his meditation is that he stands in awe at the power of God. This type of meditation is converted into action. His fruit can be identified in Galatians 5:22, 23. He meditates on the love of God, the joy of God, and the peace of God. He meditates on long-suffering when he thinks of his family. He meditates on gentleness when he thinks of those who sold him into slavery. He meditates on goodness while in prison, and on faith, meekness, and temperance while he is a leader in Egypt. He not only meditates on the Word but is a "doer" of the Word (James 1:22).

Joseph's secret—"he lives by a well." Joseph's dream stayed alive because of his secret well. Joseph is like the tree described by the Psalmist, who wrote, "And he shall be like a tree planted by the rivers of water, that bringeth forth his fruit in his season; his leaf also shall not wither, and whatsoever he doeth shall prosper" (Psalm 1:3). Whenever Joseph was tested by his enemies, he would go to his well. What well, you ask? The well of worship. The well of prayer.

The wells of salvation. Isaiah called it the well of salvation. "Therefore with joy shall ye draw water out of the wells of salvation" (Isaiah 12:3). Jacob declared that Joseph survived because of his well that never runs dry.

"His branch (faith) runs over the walls (osbtacle)." Joseph encountered the wall of abuse and rejection from his brothers, but he overcame. He encountered the wall of betrayal from Potiphar's wife, but he overcame. He encountered unthankful prison inmates, but he overcame. Joseph's dreams were greater than any wall (obstacle). A dreamer cannot be stopped by walls (osbtacle). Joseph's tree branches are his dreams and his faith. His dreams run over the walls (osbtacle) of abuse, rejection, and betrayal. While in the pit his brothers trapped him in, he sees himself free from the pit. While in prison, he sees himself liberated from prison. His dreams branch out and up during times of famine. Nothing is impossible. No wall is too high for him to climb.

3) The secret dreams of his enemies. "The archers have sorely grieved him, and shot at him, and hated him" (Genesis 49:23). Jacob declared that Joseph would experience grief in his life. Jacob called these enemies and sources of grief "archers." The archers did three things—first they grieved Joseph, second they shot at him, and third they hated him.

Secret grief. The archers were his brothers who sold him into slavery. Joseph experienced the pain of rejection, yet Joseph kept his grief secret. He never said "my no-good brothers have betrayed me." He told only God of his pain and disappointment. Through God, Jacob understood Joseph's life of struggles. "The archers have sorely grieved him."

A super-dysfunctional family. It is painful when your family becomes "super-dysfunctional." I define a super-dysfunctional family as a family who rejects you and intentionally attempts to harm you. Joseph was grieved because his brothers were super-dysfunctional and persecuted him without a cause. He was grieved because he loved his brothers and they hated him. He was grieved because his brothers rejected God. "I beheld the transgressors, and was grieved; because they kept not thy word" (Psalm 119:158).

Secret shots. The archer was Potiphar's wife who falsely accused Joseph of attempted rape. Potiphar's wife played a small but well-known role in Joseph's life. While Potiphar was out of town on a long journey, his wife tried to seduce Joseph. This, of course, was done by her in secret. Joseph refused her sexual advances—his dreams were greater than a one-night stand with Mrs. Potiphar. Joseph replied, "How can I do this great wickedness, and sin against God?" (Genesis 39:9). When Potiphar returned home, his wife reported the incident to her husband, but she took a cheap shot by falsely accusing Joseph of trying to rape her. Joseph was imprisoned for this false accusation. "They shoot in secret at the perfect: suddenly do they shoot at him, and fear not." (Psalm 64:4). Secret attacks cannot destroy a man or woman with a God-given dream.

Secret hatred. Secret hatred is designed to rob us of our secret dreams. Concealed hatred is often found in people who are the closest to us. It can be found in our own family, close relatives, and close friends. The hatred is secret because the person does not want to be exposed for whatever reason. Joseph was loved by his father but hated by his brothers. The archer was the "spiritual wickedness" or the "devil" that captured the hearts of the men and women who hated Joseph. Who knows the depths and breadth of demonic forces against the righteous? How does one develop hatred? Where does it come from?

4) The secrets of Joseph's victory. "But his bow abode in strength, and the arms of his hands were made strong by the hands of the mighty God of Jacob (from thence is the shepherd, the stone of Israel)" (Genesis 49:24). Here, Jacob declared that there were three things that would save Joseph. They would be his bow, the shepherd, and the stone.

The secrets of his bow and arrow. Jacob uttered that Joseph's bow would aid him. Jacob was referring to Joseph's faith. Jacob said, "The arms of his hands were made strong by the hands of the mighty God of Jacob." His God-given dreams were stronger than his imagination. The secret of Joseph's bow was his secret dreams. "And they said unto him, We have dreamed a dream, and there is no interpreter of it. And Joseph said unto them, Do not interpretations belong to God? tell me them, I pray you" (Genesis 40:8).

Joseph's weapon. Joseph's dreams were his weapons. His dreams built his faith. 2 Corinthians 10:4 says, "For the weapons of our warfare are not carnal, but mighty through God to the pulling down of strong holds." Joseph put his trust in the Lord and saw the strongholds destroyed. The Psalmist declared, "For I will not trust in my bow, neither shall my sword save me. But thou hast saved us from our enemies, and hast put them to shame that hated us" (Psalm 44:6–7).

The shepherd's secret. Joseph knew God as a shepherd. Joseph dreamed about the shepherd. While in Egypt, Joseph experienced God preparing a table for him in the presence of his enemies (Psalm 23:5). A good shepherd will not turn a deaf ear to his sheep. The secret of the shepherd is that "he leads Joseph like a flock." Joseph heard the shepherd's voice—it was a voice of love and tenderness. When you hear a shepherd speak to the sheep, listen to the tone of unspeakable love. The sheep senses the power of his presence. "And the sheep hear the shepherd's voice: and he calleth his own sheep by name" (John 10:3).

Before the shepherd takes his flock across a river, he goes first to ensure safety. He trains the shepherd dogs with secret tricks for keeping his flock together. The shepherd dogs have been trained to not only point out the way but to ensure that the way is practical and safe. They ensure that no wolves are present while the flock feeds. The secret of the shepherd is to provide protection and to create an atmosphere conducive for dreaming. "Give ear, O Shepherd of Israel, thou that leadest Joseph like a flock; thou that dwellest between the cherubims, shine forth" (Psalm 80:1).

The secret of the stone. Jacob declared that the secret of Joseph's victory was a stone. Jacob called Joseph the stone of Israel (Genesis 49:24). He was an Old Testatment "living stone." 1 Peter 2:5 say, "Ye also, as lively stones, are built up a spiritual house, an holy priesthood, to offer up spiritual sacrifices, acceptable to God by Jesus Christ." The secret of the stone is that it is alive!

- When his brothers betrayed him and stole his coat, Jacob said, "he found a living stone."

- When his brothers threw him in a pit, Jacob said, "he found a living stone in the pit!"

- When his brothers sold him into slavery, Jacob said, "he found a living stone in slavery!"

- When Potiphar's wife tempted him, Jacob said, "he found a living stone when she lied on him!"

- When he was imprisoned on false charges, Jacob said, "he found a living stone in prison!"

- The living stone was the revelation of his God. The secret of the living stone is Christ. Christ is the living stone—the tried, elected, and precious stone which God appointed from of old. Psalm 118:22 declares, "The stone which the builders refused is become the head stone of the corner."

5) The secrets of a threefold blessing. "Even by the God of thy father, who shall help thee; and by the Almighty, who shall bless thee with blessings of heaven above, blessings of the deep that lieth under, blessings of the breasts, and of the womb" (Genesis 49:25).

Jacob's benediction on his sons was a prophetic treasure. God promised Joseph an abundant life, and Jacob pronounced a threefold blessing. First a heavenly blessing for his soul, second an earthly blessing for his finances, and third a physical blessing for his health. This prophecy runs parallel with 3 John 2, which states, "Beloved, I wish above all things that thou mayest prosper and be in health, even as thy soul prospereth."

The secrets of the blessings of heaven (soul). "Even by the God of thy father, who shall help thee; and by the Almighty, who shall bless thee with blessings of heaven above" (Genesis 49:25). Jacob declared the blessings of heaven. Blessings from heaven are God's mercy and truth. Jacob wanted Joseph to remain steadfast in mercy and truth. Psalm 57:3 declares, "He shall send from heaven, and save from the reproach of him that would swallow me up. Selah. God shall send forth his mercy and his truth."

The secrets of earthly blessing (prosperity). "Blessings of the deep that lieth under" (Genesis 49:25). Jacob declared that secret, hidden "blessings of the deep" would be revealed. This prosperity was secret prosperity. It resided in a secret place in the spirit realm. Matthew 6:33 says, "But seek ye first the kingdom of God, and his righteousness; and all these things shall be added unto you." These blessings are small seeds of faith. They are unseen but will flourish in the right season.

The secret blessings of the breast and womb (body). "Blessings of the breasts, and of the womb"(Genesis 49:25). When you are waiting for test results from a search for breast or prostate cancer, you must remember that God will always give hope. The believer is never in a hopeless situation. The breasts of grace are full of consolation and peace. Of the hope that flows from the breast of God, Isaiah 66:11 declares, "That ye may suck, and be satisfied with the breasts of her consolations; that ye may milk out, and be delighted with the abundance of her glory." Jacob declares to Joseph the blessings of the "breasts and womb" of God. Rachel, Joseph's mother, was once barren, but God healed her and gave her a testimony. What an awesome testimony! Psalm 22:9 states, "But thou art he that took me out of the womb: thou didst make me hope when I was upon my mother's breasts." Secret dreams of the ancestors "prevailed above the blessings of my progenitors."

The Secret of Daddy's blessing. "The blessings of thy father have prevailed above the blessings of my progenitors (ancestors) unto the utmost bound of the everlasting hills" (Genesis 49:26). Jacob reminds Joseph of his forefathers' blessings (Abraham and Isaac). He stated that their blessings are still in force. Jacob compared the blessings to the hill of Israel. Jacob tells Joseph that his blessings are greater than his father and grandfather, Abraham and Isaac. Jacob receives a greater blessing because through his son he can foresee the coming of the messiah. What are these blessings that have been passed down from generation to generation?

Blessing on his head. "They shall be on the head of Joseph" (Genesis 49:26). These are generational blessings bestowed upon Abraham, Isaac, Jacob, Joseph, and the Christian family. Jacob declared that God placed these blessings on the head of Joseph, which refers to the exaltation of Joseph. It typifies Christ. Genesis 49:26 says, "And on the crown of the head of him that was separate from his brethren." Placing these attributes upon his head denoted power, authority, glory, solidity, and honor. "For thou go before him with the blessings of goodness: thou settest a crown of pure gold on his head" (Psalm 21:3).

The secret of Joseph is that he's a type of Christ. Joseph was a type of Christ. Everything that Joseph did was something to help us in our understanding of Christ. Much of the dealings with Joseph and Jesus were performed in secrecy. The parallels below provide similar experiences of these two men.

1. **Secret hatred, made public.** Joseph was despised by his own brothers (Genesis 37: 4). Jesus was despised by his own brothers, the Jews (John 1:11).

2. **Silver exchanged in secret— the price of a slave.** Joseph was sold for twenty pieces of silver (Genesis 37: 28). Jesus was sold for thirty pieces of silver (Matthew 26:15).

3. **Secret strategies of Judah and Judas.** Judah was responsible for selling Joseph (Genesis 37:27). Judas (New Testament name for Judah) was responsible for betraying Jesus (Matthew 26: 14–15).

4. **Family secrets**. Joseph's own family wanted to kill him (Genesis 37:17–20). Jesus' own family (Jewish nation) wanted to kill him (John 7:1, 11:53).

5. **Secret proceedings of the Gentiles**. Joseph was turned over to the Gentiles (Genesis 37:27). Jesus was turned over to the Gentiles (Mark 15:1).

6. **Secrets of the army**. Joseph was placed under the dominion of an officer in the strongest army in the world (Potiphar of Egypt) (Genesis 37:36). Jesus was placed under the dominion of an officer in the strongest army in the world (Pilate of Rome) (Mark 15:1).

7. **Secrets of hell**. Potiphar sentenced Joseph to the king's prison (a special prison for people who sinned against the king) (Genesis 39:20). Pilate sentenced Jesus to death; in death he went to hell (a special prison for people who sin against the King) (Mark 15:15; Acts 2:29–32).

8. **Secret of the prisoners**. Joseph was given power over all the prisoners who were in prison (Genesis 39:22–23). God gave Jesus power over hell and all that was in it (Revelations 1:18; 1 Peter 3:18–20).

9. **Secrets of the malefactors**. There were two malefactors (the butler and the baker) who were sentenced to prison— one lived and the other died (Genesis. 40:21–22). There were two malefactors during the sentencing of Jesus (two thieves)—one found eternal life, the other found eternal death (Luke 23:32–33; 39–43).

10. **Secret of the resurrection**. Pharaoh set Joseph free and gave him a change of raiment (Genesis 41:14). God raised Jesus from the dead, and glorified his resurrected body (1 Corinthians 15:20).

11. **Secret of exaltation**. Pharaoh was so pleased with Joseph that he made him lord over everything (Genesis. 41:39–44). God made Jesus Lord over everything (1 Peter 3:22; Ephesians1:20; 1 Corinthians 15:24–28).

12. **Secret of lordship**. Pharaoh commanded every knee to bow before Joseph (Genesis 41:43). God has commanded every knee to bow before Jesus (Philippians 2:9–10).

13. **Secret of a name**. Pharaoh gave Joseph the name Zaphnathpaaneah, which means "savior" (Genesis 41:45). God gave Jesus his name, and his name means "savior" (Matthew. 1:21).

14. **Secrets of the brides**. Pharaoh gave Joseph a Gentile bride (Genesis. 41:45). God gave Jesus a Gentile bride (Ephesians. 5:3).

15. **The "timing" secrets of ministry**. Joseph was thirty years old when he started making provision (Genesis 41:46). Jesus was thirty years old when he began his ministry (Luke 3:22–23).

16. **Secret of sufficiency**. Joseph buys everything with bread from the people; their secret possessions; their lands. After having received all, he gives all to Pharaoh (Genesis 47:11–23). Jesus buys everything with his blood. Then he gives it all to the King, God the Father (1 Corinthians 15:24–28).

POINTS TO PONDER

The Secret of Joseph—Secret Dreams. Joseph was the eleventh son of Jacob. His name means "add"— added vision, added dreams. His mother's name was Rachel. He represents people who have secret dreams. Joseph got in trouble with his brothers because he told his dreams prematurely. However, his dreams were benefical in Egypt because, through God's divine providence, Jacob came to realize the purpose of his dreams. While in Egypt, Pharaoh changed Joseph's name to Zaphnath-paaneah, which means "revealer of secrets". Have you told someone your secret dream only to find that the more you exposed it the more you lost the desire to do it? Do you have big plans? Are you planning to build a house, start a business or new career, home-schooling your child, or beginning a new branch of ministry? Well, if you have a dream, you cannot tell everyone. Dreams are like processing film—if the film is exposed too soon, you can destroy your picture. Keep your mouth shut! Work out the details of your dream on your own until your spirit says it is time to reveal it. Jacob prophesied that Joseph and his family would display the characteristics of a fruit vine.

- The power of a dream cannot be released until you wake up, plan, and connect it with action.

- Dreaming is one method by which God communicates with us.

- If there is conflict between a dream and Scripture, Scripture must take precedent. Never put a dream above Scripture.

- A dream without interpretation is meaningless.

- When you are faced with sickness and physical challenges, a dream can give you the energy to fight.

- Sharing your dreams with the wrong folks can be unproductive and sometimes counterproductive.

- Sharing dreams should be limited to a "trusted few" and kept secret at the infancy stage.

- Dreams can encourage and aid people in getting through difficult times.

- Your God-given dreams must be stronger than your imagination.

- Secret attacks cannot destroy a man or a woman with a God-given dream.

Joseph knew the power of unlocking dreams, yet his brother Benjamin could never unlock the riches of his own character. Let us look at the last son, Benjamin, and his secret insecurity.

CHAPTER 12

THE SECRET OF BENJAMIN

SECRET INSECURITY

"Benjamin shall ravin as a wolf: in the morning he shall devour the prey, and at night he shall divide the spoil" (Genesis 49:27).

As a little boy, I remember watching a movie called "The Wolf Man." The best version of "The Wolf Man" was produced in 1941. These movies featured actors like Lon Chaney, Jr., and Bela Lugosi who played innocent, gentle citizens who turned into werewolves. The movies were very scary and popular. Here is a plot summary: The lead character has a warm personality—he is easy to be with. However, when the moon is full, the character grows long teeth and hair, gets angry, and rips people apart. He cannot help it. He is a good person, but he was cursed. He would once again assume a human form at the break of day.

What fascinated me about the wolf man was his multiple personalities. He appeared to have schizophrenia. *Webster's Dictionary* defines schizophrenia as "a psychotic disorder characterized by loss of contact with the environment, by noticeable deterioration in the level of functioning in everyday life." Common characteristics of schizophrenia are delusions, hallucinations, disorganized speech, grossly disorganized or catatonic behavior, a limited ability to express emotions and feelings, a lack of interest or energy unaccompanied by depressed affect, and an inability to sustain concentration or attention. Wolf man was schizophrenic. He had two personalities. One personality was glamorous, secure, charitable, charming, and winning, and the other personality was delusional, insecure, vindictive, barbaric, and evil. What is really sad about the wolf man story was that he was never cured. As we read a little about Benjamin's childhood and life, we will see the patterns of a wolf man. We are living in a society full of people who are like the wolf man—they have two personalities. If you are planning on getting married make sure the person you are marrying does not have a secret personality.

Some couples feel that changing their names after marriage signifies the melding of two personalities but sometime the marriage is the melding of three personalities. It is a terrible thing to get married, return from your honeymoon, and soon discover that the person you have married is a wolf covered in sheep skin. To avoid this, let us talk about dating.

Dating - how to identify a wolf. Most people should give themselves time to determine if they are dating a wolf or a sheep. I heard someone say that the purpose of dating is to collect data. If you are dating then you must collect as much information as possible. This information should help you to determine if could live with this person for the rest of your life. The prophet declared, "Can two walk together, except they be agreed?" (Amos 3:3).

A wolf in sheep's clothing. Sometimes people use religion to bait another person into a relationship. They pretend to be religious and act sanctimonious. They have two personalities. They have a religious persona that is perfect and another personality that is a "work in progress." They tend to attract you with that perfect persona, but do not get caught marrying that perfect personality. Dating gives you time to discover secrets, and such privileged information will help you determine whether or not the person you are dating is a wolf in sheep's clothing.

The purpose of dating. Dating allows you time to discover the secrets of your lover. Secrets must be revealed (good and bad) in every relationship. If you are dating, you should find out as much as possible about the person you are dating before marrying them, which is why premarital counseling is so important. I would highly advise couples to seek at least six to twelve months of premarital counseling before marriage. Premarital counseling allows you time to discover your fiancé's secrets. It allows you time to determine if they have a bad temper, if they are stingy and unforgiving, or if they are unable to communicate. Dating gives you time to discover your lover's habits (good and bad), and then you can make a determination as to whether you can live with this person (wolf man/wolf woman) for the rest of your life.

Secret insecurity. What is insecurity? According to *Webster's Dictionary*, insecurity is a mental state in which one demonstrates behaviors of inferiority and low self-confidence. Insecure peeople are:

- more easily offended than those with self-confidence.

- more likely to be suspicious of others.

- control oriented; the power they receive from being in control of others feed that need.

- afraid to take risks.

- afraid to risk building up others with compliments, because they are constantly in need of compliments themselves.

• those who always have to be right at everything.

Your secret weaknesses (known and unknown) are the foundation of secret insecurities. In order to get rid of your secret insecurity you must express your weaknesses, confront them, and give your secret faults and weaknesses to Christ (1 Peter 5:7). Tell God about your secret sins and identify your specific secret insecurities. The spirit of insecurity takes root when your secret faults are not exposed. Oh, how we need Jesus! The Psalmist cried, "Cleanse me from secret faults" (Psalm 19:12).

The Jekyll and Hyde spirit. Let us turn our attention to the last son, Benjamin. Benjamin is a symbolic representation of people who have split or multiple personalities. Benjamin is like Dr. Jekyll and Mr. Hyde. Robert Louis Stevenson's fictional story of Jekyll and Hyde is about good and evil. The names and the story are so popular today that it is synonymous with split-personality behavior. Dr. Jekyll was a wealthy, quiet, handsome, honorable, and distinguished man, but he was obsessed with the idea that different entities could occupy one man's body. He created a potion that transformed him into the ugly Edward Hyde and allowed him to commit whatever crime or social depravity he wished without feeling the shame that Dr. Jekyll would feel.

Benjamin represents people with a "good side" and an "ugly side." Aristotle said, "No excellent soul is exempt from a mixture of madness." With Benjamin, one personality is outgoing, friendly, and accepting, and the other personality is reclusive, unfriendly, and judgmental.

Prophecy from the bedside. Jacob declared that Benjamin would be a ravenous wolf that would destroy his enemies (Genesis 49:27). Moses declared a gentler side of his personality, however, and portrayed him as a gentle lamb on the shoulders of his shepherd (Deuteronomy 33:12). What a dichotomy! Benjamin is characterized as a boy with secret insecurities. People with secret insecurities are dangerous. They are unpredictable. Benjamin's insecurities are revealed in Jacob's final prophecy.

1) A boy with two names—secret identity crisis
2) The mysteries of death
3) Moses' prophecy about Benjamin

1) A boy with two names—secret identity crisis. Figure 12.1 shows that Benjamin was Jacob's twelfth son. He was Rachel's second son and also the only son born in Canaan. His mother died while giving birth to him. Benjamin was born into a difficult situation—he had no nurse, no mother, and no grandmother. Rachel was the first mother in the Bible to die while giving birth to a child. With her last breath, Rachel named her son "Benoni," proclaiming, "You are the cause of my sorrow." Can you imagine the stigma and the teasing Benoni would receive as a youth? In the midst of multiple contractions, bleeding, sweating, and tears, Rachel screamed, "Benoni! Benoni! Benoni!"

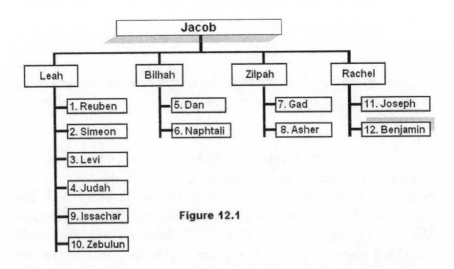

Figure 12.1

Rachel's words were as prophetic as her pain. As she pushed for the last time and watched her little, wet infant slip from her bruised womb, she named her son "Benoni," which means, "son of sorrow" (Genesis 35:19). Jacob did not agree with this name and quickly renamed his son Benjamin, which means, "son of my right hand." It was too late, however, to wipe the name from history, and it should be noted that Benjamin was the only son named by his father. As Rachel lay there dying, Jacob shouted, "No, we shall not call him Benoni. We shall call him Benjamin," his new, favored son. Here we see the beginning of secret insecurities—it started with a boy with two names.

A reason for a name change. Jacob changed his son's name because he knew that a name can determine a destiny. Would the community remember and remind Benjamin that his mother died while calling him the "son of her sorrow"? How would that impact him? Would it cause him to encounter an identity crisis? God renamed several people. Many men and women in the Bible were given new names by the Lord. Some notable name changes in the Bible are:

- Abram became Abraham (Genesis 17:5).
- Sarai became Sarah (Genesis 17:15).
- Jacob became Israel (Genesis 32:28).
- Simon-Cephas became Peter (Matthew 10:2).
- Saul of Tarsus became the Apostle Paul (Acts 13:9).

The names listed above were changed for special reasons. God changed their names because he was calling them to a new life and a new identity.

When Jesus Christ calls us to follow him, we leave our old life behind and become a new person in Christ. The new creature we become receives a new name, which is revealed to us by God. The purpose of the new name is to separate us from our old life of bondage. We are not the same person after Jesus Christ calls us out of the world to be his ambassadors. "Therefore if any man be in Christ, he is a new creature: old things are passed away; behold, all things are become new" (2 Corinthians 5:17).

Saul was from the tribe of Benjamin and was called to be the first king of Israel. The tribe of Benjamin represents people who are insecure and are always uncertain of their purpose. They do not know what to believe about themselves or their future. Saul was the first example of an insecure king. When called to be king he said, "Am not I a Benjamite, of the smallest of the tribes of Israel? And my family the least of all the families of the tribe of Benjamin? Wherefore then speakest thou so to me?" (1 Samuel 9:21). We again see the insecurities of this Benjamite when Samuel publicly presented him as the new king of Israel. The Bible says he "hid himself among the stuff [baggage]" (1 Samuel 10:22). Let us look closer at this response. When Samuel called Saul to his new kingly responsibilities, Saul responded in the following fashion:

- "Am not I a Benjamite"—inferiority.

- "From the smallest tribe"—insignificance.

- "My family is the least of the smallest tribe" —inadequacy.

- "Why are you speaking to me" —incredibility.

- "He hid himself among the stuff"—inaccessibility.

King Saul was an insecure leader. Insecure people are easily offended. Insecure people are also afraid to try anything new, they fear change, they are afraid to make decisions, and they are afraid of confrontation.

From little to tiny. Saul did a good job at first of being king of Israel, but his feelings of inferiority, insignificance, inadequacy, incredibility, and inaccessibility later played a crucial part in his downfall. Benjamin is called "little" in the Psalm. The Psalmist declared, "There is *little* Benjamin with their ruler, the princes of Judah and their council, the princes of Zebulun, and the princes of Naphtali" (Psalm 68:27). Why did God refer to Benjamin as "little?"

- Little numerically—he had the smallest tribe in Israel (1 Samuel 9:21).

- Little territorially—his land was very small in comparison.

- Little influence—his influence on the other tribes was insignificant in comparison to the other tribes.

Because of his insecurity, King Saul took things into his own hands in offering sacrifices and circumventing the commands of God (1 Samuel 12:13–14, 15:10–31). The exalted position of the monarchy was too much for him to handle. He abused his power as King.

The insecurity of Saul of Tarsus. Apostle Paul was a descendent of the tribe of Benjamin. Paul is first presented in the Bible as a killer of Christians. Before adopting the name Apostle Paul, he was Saul of Tarsus. Saul of Tarsus was a well-educated man, and he was very dedicated to his faith. He dedicated his life to enforcing the Mosaic Law. When someone violated the Torah, Saul would ensure that the person was punished. Therefore when Christian Jews converted to Christ, Saul of Tarsus sought to kill these people for their conversion.

On the road to Damascus to persecute Christians in that city, Saul met Jesus and experienced a conversion. He was transformed by this encounter. He was a changed man. He went into seclusion for three years to study this new revelation of Christ (Galatians 1:18). He had to get rid of his old habits and find a new way of thinking. Saul the killer of Christians was soon Paul the champion of the Christian faith.

Jesus' identity is challenged. Jesus was called many names. The prophets called him Emmanuel (Isaiah 7:14; Matthew 1:23), but his parents called him Jesus. Satan took advantage of his multiple names and titles and challenged Jesus' identity. Was Jesus the "son of man" or "son of God"? Was Jesus Benoni, "a son of sorrow" as recorded in

Isaiah 53:3? Or was he "the son who sits on the right hand side of the father" as recorded in Revelation 1:17; Psalm 80:17, 89:21; and Acts 5:31?

In Matthew 4:3 Satan tested the identity of Jesus. He said, "If thou be the Son of God, command that these stones be made bread." On three occasions Satan questioned the identity of Jesus by asking, "If thou be the Son of God." The "if" question was complex because it seemed Satan was asking Jesus, "Are you a man of sorrow or are you the righteousness of God? Exactly who are you?"

Are you Superman or Clark Kent? Satan challenged the humanity and divinity of Jesus. Satan was saying, "If you are a man then act like a man. If you are a god then act like a god. Are you Superman or Clark Kent? Who are you, Jesus?"

Satan asked, "If thou be the Son (humanity) of God (divinity), then do a miracle!" Like a lawyer making a closing argument to the jurors, Satan attempted to create doubt and uncertainty in the mind of Jesus. Even in the twenty-first century Satan questions the identity of every Christian believer. Christian believers who are secretly insecure about their faith in Christ are easily shaken (2 Thessalonians 2:2). The Apostle Paul wrote, "Nevertheless I am not ashamed: for I know whom I have believed, and am persuaded that he is able to keep that which I have committed unto him against that day" (2 Timothy 1:12).

2) The mysteries of death.

Request for an autopsy. For Jacob, Rachel's death was a mystery. She died from complications. Benjamin had to accept his mother's death. Studies show that when a mother dies after giving birth, her newborn baby has a much lower chance of surviving in his or her first year. Children who survive their mother's death are less likely to receive adequate nourishment and health care. Did Benjamin receive sufficient nourishment? Benjamin was without a mother. Who would care for him? Who would adopt him? Would it be the concubines (Bilhah and Zilpah) or Leah? Since children depend on parents and other adults to take care of them, the grieving Jacob had to find a caregiver.

Talking to children about death. Jacob is silent in Scripture about the death of Rachel. He does not explain to Benjamin why or how his mother died. I believe that Jacob had difficulty in explaining death, especially while grieving the loss of Joseph (Genesis 37:35). Our failure to cope with fear or a loss is the root cause of insecurity. As Benjamin grew up, I believe that Jacob never found the appropriate time to talk to his son, and this may have caused Benjamin to develop low self-esteem and insecurity.

When discussing death with children, explanations should be simple and direct. A child should be told the truth using as much detail as he or she is able to understand. The child's questions should be answered honestly and directly. Children need to be reassured about their own security. Children's questions should be answered with care that the child understands the answers. I believe, this never happened for Benjamin. Psychologists have proven that if a child thinks that a death could not have been prevented, the child may think that he or she could also die[10].

The death of Rachel was especially hard for Jacob. Jacob loved Rachel more than life, and Jacob was never the same after her death. I believe Benjamin was secretly asking the question, "Will I die like my mother?" Was he responsible for his father's perpetual sadness too? If so, what was going to happen to him? Did Benjamin think he was unworthy to live? Did he entertain secret thoughts of suicide or desire for death?

---

[10]   *Trozzi, Maria, Talking With Children Loss, The Berkley Publishing Group, 1991.*

The four mysteries of death. Death is not a secret. Death is a mystery. To overcome his insecurity, Benjamin needed to accept the four mysteries of death. To those of us who are Christians, the mystery of death is solved by the death and resurrection of Jesus Christ. The Christian finds security in knowing Christ has conquered death. The Apostle wrote, 1 Corinthians 15:19, "If in this life only we have hope in Christ, we are of all men most miserable."

1. **The secret of overcoming the "reality of death"**. The first mystery Benjamin had to face was the reality of death. The reality of death is difficult to deal with for both adults and children. The reality of death is said to be a source of freedom. Death is not a joke. Death is not a dream. Death is not a fairytale. By accepting our mortality, we can free ourselves from the bondage of fear and ignorance. When we acknowledge death as inevitable instead of being blinded by our fear of it, everything else just comes into clearer focus.

   Paul writes of two deaths, saying, "And as it is appointed unto men once to die, but after this the judgment" (Hebrews 9:27). The passing of a soul into a state of nonexistence or other existence is a mystery. Death is real, and the reality of death is indeed mysterious. Yet Jesus challenged the reality of death and gave hope. Jesus said, "If a man keep my saying, he shall never taste of death" (John 8:52). Jesus reverses the reality of death. Jesus promises everlasting life. Jesus said, "For God so loved the world, that he gave his only begotten Son, that whosoever believeth in him should not perish, but have everlasting life" (John 3:16).

2. **The secret of overcoming the "finality of death"**. Second, Benjamin had to accept the finality of death. Death is final. The finality of death affects different people different ways. It is irreversible. Benjamin must accept the finality of his mother's death. Benjamin would grow

up understanding his mother would never be a part of his life. He would hear stories about his brother, Joseph (whom Jacob presumed dead). Death is rarely a welcomed guest. No matter what the illness, no matter how long the suffering has taken place, the finality of death is hard for anyone to bear.

The story of Lazarus, as recorded for us in John chapter 11, tells of Jesus raising Lazarus from the dead after several days in his tomb. It was difficult for Lazarus' sisters, Mary and Martha to accept the death of their brother, Lazarus. The fear of permanent separation from everyone and everything is the hallmark of death. The fear of eternal nothingness, eternal separation, or the unknown is hard to accept. "Lazarus is dead," Jesus says starkly, and he was right! Lazarus was in the tomb for four days—long enough for there to be a stench. Lazarus was dead. Yet Jesus overcame the finality of death, and because of Jesus death is no longer final. "Jesus said unto her, I am the resurrection, and the life: he that believeth in me, though he were dead, yet shall he live ..." (John 11:25). Only Jesus has the ability to reverse death. "The last enemy that shall be destroyed is death" (1 Corinthians 15:26)

3. **The secret of overcoming the "rationality of death."** Third, Benjamin had to cease from rationalizing death. When faced with death, Benjamin had to avoid asking himself over and over, "Why Lord? Why?" Death is irrational—it never makes sense. It just happens. It happens to good and righteous men and women. So Benjamin needed to say "Amen" and keep looking to the future. He could not afford to rationalize Rachel's death. He had to simply accept it.

Death never comes at the perfect time or the perfect location. Death is untimely and imperfect, and we seem to never get accustomed to it. Yet, Paul addresses the matter of death. He writes that death is swallowed by the victory of Calvary (1 Corinthians 15:54). Because of the death, resurrection, and promise of Christ's return, death does not have to be understood. "O death, where is thy sting? O grave, where is thy victory?" (1 Corinthians 15:55).

4. **The secret of understanding the "locality of death".** Fourth, death takes us out of this world and ushers us to a new place or locality. When a person dies, what happens to his or her soul? Benjamin had to address the issue of Rachel's locality and understand where her soul resided. Was it in the bosom of Abraham? Was it in torment? Was it sleeping in an unconscious state? Was it nonexistent? Paul answers this question when he said, "We are confident, I say, and willing rather to be absent from the body, and to be present with the Lord" (2 Corinthians 5:8).

A father who could not be comforted. The Bible is silent regarding Benjamin's encouragement. He seemed to be a boy who lived in an environment absent of affirmations. Until Jacob visited Egypt, he refused to comfort himself or others. "And all his sons and all his daughters rose up to comfort him; but he **refused to be comforted**; and he said, For I will go down into the grave unto my son mourning. Thus his father wept for him" (Genesis 37:35). It is easy to feel insecure. Jacob seemed to be locked in a state of depression because of the alleged death of Joseph and the death of Rachel.

The personalities for the morning and night. Jacob said, "In the morning he shall devour the prey at night he shall divide the spoil" (Genesis 49:27). Here, Jacob declared two types of behaviors. During the day, Benjamin "devours or destroys" and at night he shares his spoils. He is portrayed as sharing goods taken from the enemy after a battle (Ephesians 4:7-8, Psalm 68:18, 1 Corinthians 15:55-57).

Benjamin's activities in the day. While lying on his deathbed, Jacob described Benjamin as a ravenous wolf. Moses, however, described him as a lamb. Here again we see this dichotomous personality. Jacob predicted that Benjamin would "devour" his enemies in the morning. Notice that Jacob cited the early hours of the day—possibly one or three in the morning—that Benjamin would roam the streets seeking to kill. Benjamin knew that the early bird gets the worm. Jacob stated that he "shall devour." "Devour" means to eat up greedily or ravenously. It means to "seize upon and destroy" like a warrior in battle. Jacob knew that Benjamin and his family, though insecure, would have a warlike personality.

Benjamin's activities at night. Jacob foretold that at night Benjamin would "divide the spoil." At night Benjamin would show another side of his personality. In the morning he is a devourer, but at night he is a divider. "Divide" suggests Benjamin's ability to reason, to distinguish right from wrong, and to separate. Benjamin would divide the spoil, which represents the loot (goods of considerable value) taken from an enemy in war or robbery.

3) Moses' prophecy about Benjamin. "And of Benjamin he said, The beloved of the LORD shall dwell in safety by him; and the LORD shall cover him all the day long, and he shall dwell between his shoulders" (Deuteronomy 33:12).

In Deuteronomy 33:12, Moses blessed the tribe of Benjamin. Moses described Benjamin as a lamb that dwells in safety between its shepherd's shoulders. It is not uncommon for a shepherd to carry sheep on their shoulders, and like Moses, Jesus gave a vivid picture of a shepherd carrying sheep on his shoulders (Luke 15:5). Moses declared that the tribe of Benjamin was, "Beloved of the LORD." Benjamin was the last son of Jacob but "beloved of the Lord." Benjamin was a son without a mother but "beloved of the Lord." He had two personalities, but he was "beloved of the Lord." Benjamin was called the beloved of the Lord, and so was Jesus (Luke 3:22).

In spite of Benjamin's low-self esteem and insecurity, Moses declared that Benjamin "shall dwell in safety." Moses was saying that as you devour your prey in the morning you will dwell in safety. And as you divide the spoils of your victory at night, you shall also dwell in safety. Moses painted a wonderful picture of a father wrapping an insecure child in a warm blanket. Moses said, "The LORD shall cover him all the day long." God would put Benjamin on his shoulders and carry him: "he shall dwell between his shoulders." If you feel anxiety and insecurity, God wants to carry you on his shoulders. "Casting all your cares upon him; for he careth for you" (1 Peter 5:7).

POINTS TO PONDER

The Secret of Benjamin—Secret Insecurity. Benjamin was the twelfth son of Jacob. His name means "son of my right hand". His mother was Rachel. As she was dying while giving birth to him, Rachel named him "Benoni", which means, "son of my sorrow". But his father named him Benjamin which means "son of my right hand". This meant Benjamin had two names. He also had two personalities. He represents people who appear publicly secure but are secretly insecure. He is borderline paranoid-schizophrenic. Jacob prophesied that Benjamin and his family would be like the wolf.

- Dating gives you time to discover if you are seeing a person who is a wolf in sheep's clothing.

- Dating allows you time to discover the secrets of your lover.

- Benjamin represents people who are insecure.

- The first sign of Benjamin's secret insecurities was his name.

- Insecurity is a mental state in which one demonstrates behaviors of inferiority and low self-confidence.

- The spirit of insecurity takes root when your secret faults are not exposed.

- Our failure to cope with fear or loss is the root cause to insecurity.

- To those of us who are Christians, the mystery of death is not a mystery at all, for we are secure in God. The mystery of death is solved in the life Jesus.

- Wrong living, secret sin, and not being right with God (living under a dark, impending cloud) are causes of deep insecurities.

- All of us need affirmations and encouragement.

- When discussing death with children, explanations should be simple and direct.

- All of us have insecurity to some degree or another.

EPILOGUE

The *Power of Secrets* is a non-fiction allegory that portrays real biblical characters that symbolize various levels of secrecy. This section of the book was written to help you understand the power of secrets and how to cope with them. As we approach this relevant subject we must consider several factors regarding secrets:

   I. The definition of secrets
   II. The secret of eternity
   III. The power of secrets

I. The Definition of Secrets

There is a big difference between a secret and a mystery. *Webster's Dictionary* defines a secret as, "something kept hidden or something kept from the knowledge of others or shared only confidentially with a few." A secret is something decipherable and known to only a few people. In contrast, a mystery is something simply unknowable and unexplainable. *Webster's Dictionary* defines a mystery as, "something not understood or beyond understanding." Paul wrote to Timothy (1 Timothy 3:16) about the mystery of godliness, noting that, "great is the mystery of godliness ..." Paul was unable to define the substance and nature of God so he called godliness a mystery. The concept and substance of God is a mystery. Table 1 shows the differences between a secret and a mystery.

Secret	Mystery
Information hidden, suppressed but knowable.	Information inaccessible. Cannot be known.
Information is intentionally concealed by someone.	No one has the information.
After it is understood it may be held a secret.	Anything not understood is a mystery.
Problem can be solved, if released.	Problem cannot be solved.

Table 1

It is the glory of God to create the unknown, or mysteries, but he delights when a matter is transformed from a mystery into a secret. The book of Proverbs makes this point clear, stating, "It is the glory of God to conceal a thing: but the honour of kings is to search out a matter" (Proverbs 25:2–3).

The first mystery. The first mystery was unveiled in the Garden of Eden, where we saw man's first attempt to unfold the mysteries of God. The first mystery was, "good and evil." The serpent told Eve that God was keeping secrets from her. He suggested that if she ate from the forbidden tree, "Ye shall be as gods, knowing good and evil" (Genesis 3:5). The phrase, "good and evil," refers to the mysteries of God. Eve desired to know information about God that was inaccessible. The serpent told her the information was accessible. He lied! Only Christ at Calvary tasted "good and evil." Eve wanted revelations and wanted her "eyes to open" to God's mysteries. "For God doth know that in the day ye eat thereof, then your eyes shall be opened, and ye shall be as gods, knowing good and evil" (Genesis 3:5).

The second mystery. The second mystery was the coming of Christ. The serpent, which was the devil, was told of the coming birth of Christ. Genesis 3:15 (AV) reads, "And I will put enmity between thee and the woman, and between thy seed and her seed; it shall bruise thy head, and thou shalt bruise his heel." However, the devil did not understand the mystery and time of Christ's birth. It was kept a secret from him. No one knew the exact time Christ would appear. The angels did not know. The demons did not know. Only the wise men from the east were given insight to the Messiah's birthplace and birth date. Galatians 4:4 (AV) states, "But when the fullness of the time was come, God sent forth his Son, made of a woman, made under the law." Even the wise men kept the birthplace of Christ a secret from King Herod. An angel told the wise men to keep the location of Jesus a secret and not return to Herod. When the wise men failed to return to King Herod, Herod responded by killing a whole generation of children under two years old. To escape King Herod's genocide, an angel instructed Joseph to take Jesus to Africa and to remain there until King Herod dies (Matthew 2:15-17). Not even God, who is all-powerful, overlooked the power and subtly of Satan's potential attacks on Jesus.

Earth's best kept secret. For hundreds of years, the saints waited for the promised redeemer. Some died in faith waiting for his return. Everything about the coming of the redeemer was shrouded in secrecy. Why was it kept a secret and from whom? Some things must be kept secret because if they are known before the right time it could have an adverse effect. The birth time, birthplace, and biological mother of Christ was kept a secret by God.

When Christ's birthplace was first revealed, it was not on the map, and neither was it populated. At the time of the prophecy, (that Christ was to be born in Bethlehem Ephrathah) Bethlehem was not on any map and its name was unknown. It was just a place for shepherds and wolves. The birth place of Jesus was Earth's best kept secet. The prophet Micah anticipated the place of Jesus birth when he delcared, " But thou, Bethlehem Ephratah, though thou be little among the thousands of Judah, yet out of thee shall he come forth unto me that is to be ruler in Israel; whose goings forth have been from of old, from everlasting" Micah 5:2.

Swallowing up secrets. Any subject matter relating to God exceeds the notion of secrecy. God is a mystery. He is incomprehensible. He has no form. He has no beginning and no end. God cannot be understood or known except through Christ Jesus. Only Jesus made God knowable and explainable. Thank God for Jesus! Paul wrote, "And without controversy great is the mystery of godliness: God was manifest in the flesh, justified in the Spirit, seen of angels, preached unto the Gentiles, believed on in the world, received up into glory" (1 Timothy 3:16).

It is a mystery how God was seen in the flesh. It is a mystery how THE SPIRIT was "justified in the Spirit." It is a mystery how angels visited him. It is a mystery how a Jewish man named Jesus preached to the Gentiles. It is a mystery how we beheld the glory of

God who was "received up into glory." Everything about God is a mystery, but God solved the mystery of godliness by giving us Jesus. Because of Jesus, God is accessible. All of the mysteries of God are found in Jesus. Paul wrote, "For in him dwelleth all the fullness of the Godhead bodily" (Colossians 2:9). In his divinity, Jesus expressed the mystery of God (Hebrews 1:3). In his humanity, he expressed the secrecy of sonship (Matthew 16:14).

II. The Secret of Eternity

The secret of eternity starts with God's name. The word OLAM is translated Everlasting. It contains in its meaning the idea of a secret as well as a time or age and always speaks of some passing period which runs its course and fulfills its purpose in God's dealings with man.

Secrecy starts with God. Who created God? Where did God come from? How long has he been God? How can God be omnipotent (all-powerful), omnipresent (present everywhere) and omniscient (all-knowing)? God is eternal. God is invisible (1 Timothy 1:17). The unseen God clashes with logic and reason. God and creation challenges our intelligence and academic training. God gives no explanation of his actions. Where specifically is God? You cannot walk with God until you accept his right to secrecy.

The beginning of mystery. Eternity is the beginning of mystery. What is eternity? Eternity has no beginning or end. Yet, Jesus tackled the mystery of eternity. He declared that if you believe in him you are ushered into eternity. "That whosoever believeth in him should not perish, but have eternal life" (John 3:15). Paul wrote that God has prepared a place for each of us in eternity. Even though eternity is a mystery, God has given us a glimpse of eternity as described by Apostle Paul. But it is also written, "Eye hath not seen, nor ear heard, neither have entered into the heart of man, the things which God hath prepared for them that love him. But God hath revealed them unto us by his Spirit: for the Spirit searcheth all things, yea, the deep things of God" (1 Corinthians 2:9–10).

Paul wrote that God has revealed to believers his awesome love and the "deep things of God." God controls the deep things of heaven and earth. He has the authority and power to reveal secrets of his eternal sanctuary. The Psalmist sings, "You are awesome, O God, in your sanctuary; the God of Israel gives power and strength to his people" Psalm 68:35 (NIV).

Only God is awesome. God is awesome and has right to secrecy. The word "awesome" means "in awe." We must yield to the secrecy and mystery of God before we can declare him to be awesome. Jacob Louis Waldenmaier writes in *What Has Happened to Awe?* "To say that we are in awe means that we are emotionally reduced in the presence of something vaster and more magnificent than we are[11]." (Waldenmaier, Jacob Louis *What has happened to Awe?*) Our view of reality is thus shifted through our awe of God. Everything is put in perspective for us. We have suddenly seen more clearly the truth about God's identity, and our rational faculty to reason is so dwarfed by splendor that all that comes out of our mouths is the exclamation, "Awww." A house cannot be awesome. Shoes cannot be awesome. Cars cannot be awesome. Only the mysteries and secrets of God make us exclaim "Awww."

His right to secrecy. The Bible opens with secrecy. It ends with a "sealed book" being opened and revealing the words of the triumphant Christ. In Genesis 1:1 we read, "In the beginning God created the heaven and the earth." The verse does not tell us where God came from or how long God existed. The scripture is silent on the character and essence of God. There is no attempt to explain why God created the heaven and earth, how long he waited before he created it, or how long God existed in void and darkness before the act of creation. So many facts are missing! Too many facts are missing! The secrets of God are where many people meet their greatest challenge in accepting God.

---

[11]   Waldenmaier, Jacob Louis *What has happened to Awe? Copyright © 2004 http://members.aol.com/jacoblouis/awe.htm*

God is a god of secrets. He is omniscient and in control of every secret thing. "The secret things belong unto the Lord our God: but those things which are revealed belong unto us and to our children for ever, that we may do all the words of this law" (Deuteronomy 29:29).

The birth of atheism. The subject of God is mysterious, confusing to almost all. The secrets and mysteries of God gave birth to the atheists, agnostics, and believers. The secrecy and mystery of God will either attract you or repel you. It repels an atheist. An atheist is one who believes that God does not exist and is unable to accept the secrets of God or anything that he or she cannot prove or measure. The agnostic is one who holds the view that God is a mystery and any ultimate reality of God is unknown and probably unknowable. The agnostic raises the questions of who or where God is over and over again. The believer is a person who has a firm religious faith in God. The scripture leaves the believer in total secrecy and mystery concerning the orgin of God and his creation. Therefore the believer must accept God by faith and His acts.

Secrecy—the prerequisite to faith. God created faith to help us accept and understand his secrets. One cannot have faith without accepting God's secrets. Hebrews 11:3 described this secrecy as, "Through faith we understand that the worlds were framed by the word of God, so that things which are seen were not made of things which do appear." This scripture seems to say that the invisible God took his invisible word to create something very visible. Faith and hope always operate in the sphere of secrecy. Romans 8:24 says, "Hope that is seen is not hope."

III.   The Power of Secrets

Secrets are powerful things. Rabbi Edwin Friedman, author and family therapist, claims that "Secrets are serious stuff. They are never on the side of challenge and change. In fact secrets usually function to divide, to create unnecessary estrangements as well as false companionship. Secrets distort perceptions, confusing and misleading people with information that is only part of the picture. Secrets generally function to keep anxiety at higher levels."[12]

Military secrets. Under the administration of President Bill Clinton, our government adopted a policy of secrecy that required men and woman in the military to keep their sexuality a secret. The "don't ask, don't tell" policy prohibited active-duty service members from openly acknowledging whether they were gay or lesbian. This policy created secret subcultures in the military. Several bills were introduced to eliminate the military's sexual orientation policy. However, the right to "tell all" their secrets without the fear of consequences has not changed. Due to homophobia and other objections to homosexuals in the military, the exposure of their sexual orientation will either galvanize or divide members of the U.S military.

Secrets galvanize. Secrets are powerful because they confine you to an exclusive or chosen group of individuals. When an exclusive group of people are privileged to highly classified or confidential information, it causes them to bond together. The group's loyalty to keep a matter secret causes them to become loyal to each other and to experience singleness of purpose. They form an allegiance to keep their mouths closed—gangsters pledge to never "snitch," even police officers pledge to keep certain things "off the record."

Secrets divide. Secrets can be incredibly destructive. They can divide family members by preventing open and honest relationships. When friends and relatives conceal their pain it fosters more division. The old maxim is true, "Open confession is good for the soul." An undisclosed secret can be incalculable, creating a need to lie, deceive and manipulate. Tabloids still outsell "real" newspapers and magazines by astronomical numbers because our society is mesmerized by the things that divide families, countries and nations.

---

[12]   *Edwin Friedman, Generation to Generation, New York: The Guilford Press, 1985, pp. 52-54.*

In addition to this, refusing to share a secret with someone may suggest to that person that he/she cannot be trusted. Such feelings of untrustworthiness create division. Yet some secrets are exposed just to create gossip, scandals and division. You may feel rejected when you hear confidential information from someone else, especially when the information has been intentionally kept from you. When secrets are kept from you it feeds low self-esteem and makes you suspicious. Yes, it is true – honesty is the best policy – this policy keeps us from being divided

Secrets can help promote you. Every salesperson, investor, doctor, lawyer, pastor, prophet, inventor, businessperson, etc. knows the power secrets. Even the cook at Joe's Barbecue knows the power of secrets—the success of his barbecue is the secret ingredients in his barbecue sauce. The flavor of the barbecue sauce keeps customers returning to Joe's Barbecue. Joe's barbecue sauce is difficult to replicate. As we finish eating a rib tip, we lick our fingers and lips in desperation for the last taste of that glorious sauce! We say, "Man, it sure was good." We ask, "What's in the sauce?" But the response from the cook is, "It is a secret." So your secrets can give you leverage, position and power.

Secrecy, the formula to intimacy. Intimacy is accomplished through the sharing of secrets. When two people share secrets without judging each other it creates intimacy. Intimacy means "in-to-me-see." "The secret of Jehovah is with them that fear him" (Psalm 25:14). Most of us are careful not to share our secret experiences with strangers because sharing secrets makes us feel vulnerable. One of the responsibilities of a psychiatrist, psychologist, pastor, lawyer, or counselor is to help us manage our secrets. First, they want us to become honest and intimate with ourselves. Other people consult their horoscopes, Ouija boards, and fortune tellers in desperate attempts to reveal and interpret their secrets and create personal intimacy.

Exposing your secrets. Can you imagine if every second of your life was recorded on video? Would you act differently? Imagine going to the restroom and having the paparazzi follow you in with their flashing cameras. Imagine cameras and lights focused on you while you eat your breakfast, lunch, and dinner. Would you pick into your nose while eating? Certainly, not! Would you burp in front of those lenses? Absolutely not! Would you pray before you ate? Possibly! Imagine the paparazzi and their cameras in your bedroom. Would you make love to your spouse? I do not think so because the paparazzi would have invaded your privacy. People tend to act differently when they <u>know</u> they are being watched or know their privacy has been invaded. Yet, God is always watching. He is looking and recording every behavior. No behavior can be concealed from God.

Your personality is best defined when no one is watching you. The psychology of surveillance is powerful. From department stores to spy satellites, from street intersections to school buses, surveillance cameras are appearing with increasing frequency in our society for the purpose of affecting human behavior.

Sanctified by secrecy. You are sanctified by secrets. The word "sanctified" means "to be set apart." "Sanctify" is used over seventy times in the Bible. The things of God and the people of God are "set apart" from the world and its corruption exclusively for God's purpose. The secrets of God are powerful because they create walls that sanctify you once you accept them. Your secret experiences with God cause you to behave differently—they set you apart. The prophets of the Old Testament were set apart from the populace by their secrets. "Surely the Lord God will do nothing, but he revealeth his secret unto his servants the prophets" (Amos 3:7).

The Secrets of glory. As shown in Figure 1 below, God's glory is revealed through a process. The process starts with a personal experience. God conceals his glory, but it is our responsibility to discover it. He helps us to discover his glory. Proverb says, "It is the glory of God to conceal a thing: but the honour of kings is to search out a matter" (Proverbs 25:2).

As recorded in the book of Daniel, King Nebuchadnezzar declared God to be the revealer of secrets. He said, "The king answered unto Daniel, and said, of a truth it is, that your God is a God of gods, and a Lord of kings, and a revealer of secrets, seeing thou couldest reveal this secret" (Daniel 2:47). God solves puzzles, and he seals and unseals books and he whispers in the ear. All of God's secrets lead to glory.

The first step to glory starts with an accurate interpretation of your secret experiences. Let us take a look at the glory process, pictured in the glory pyramid below.

Figure 1 The Glory Pyramid

Experiences shape our belief system. A belief system is meant to be a comprehensive network of experiences and ideas about what one thinks is absolutely real and true. What we experience is often the framework of what we believe!

Our belief system shapes our communications. We speak what we believe and our actions are a reflection of our beliefs. The Psalmist said, "I believed, therefore have I spoken: I was greatly afflicted: I said in my haste, All men are liars" (Psalm 116:10–11).

Communications determine our actions. Your words program your behavior. For example, if you visit a restaurant and the service and food was horrible you might say, "I will never go to that restaurant again." Like a computer programmer, such words program our heart to follow a specific course of action. "Death and life are in the power of the tongue: and they that love it shall eat the fruit thereof" (Proverbs 18:21).

Actions are weighed by God. Spoken words program your actions or behavior. God evaluates our words and actions. "Talk no more so exceeding proudly; let not arrogancy come out of your mouth: for the LORD is a God of knowledge, and by him actions are weighed" (1 Samuel 2:3).

All secrets are designed to transform into glory. "Whether therefore ye eat, or drink, or whatsoever ye do, do all to the glory of God" (1 Corinthians 10:31).

God judges secrets. As with the sons of Jacob, God will expose every secret activity of our lives. The Apostle Paul emphasized the certainty of judgment. In Romans 2:16 he wrote, "God will judge the secrets of men through Christ Jesus." And in Romans 14:10, 12 he stated, "We shall all stand before the judgment seat of Christ … So then every one of us shall give account of himself to God." The writer of Hebrews summed it up succinctly, saying, "It is appointed unto men once to die, but after this the judgment" (Hebrews 9:27). Now let us take a look at the multiplicity of secrets in the Bible. I invite you to a quick tour through the Secret Hall of Fame in Table 2.

Table 1

The Secret Hall of Fame

		Old Testament Secrets
1	Serpent	The serpent told Eve that God was keeping a secret from her (Genesis 3:5).
2	Eve	Eve disobeyed God in exchange to know secrets of good and evil (Genesis 2:9).
3	Adam and Eve	Adam and Eve attempted to hide themselves from the presence of the Lord by covering themselves with fig leaves (Genesis 3:7).
4	Samson	Samson was a strong man who could not keep a secret (Judges 16:6–13).
5	Ham	Ham's secret was that he saw his father's (Noah) nakedness. He secretly observed his father's nakedness and was cursed (Genesis 9:22–25).
6	Bathsheba	Bathsheba kept secrets from her husband, Uriah. Her affair with David was kept secret. She kept her pregnancy a secret from her husband (2 Samuel 11:5).
7	David	David kept a secret from the prophet (Nathan). But Nathan the prophet-pastor finds out about the adultery and the secret conspiracy that killed Uriah (2 Samuel 12:7).
8	Uriah	Uriah delivered a secret message to Joab. The message to Joab was to ensure Uriah would be killed in battle (2 Samuel 11:14–18).
9	Queen of Sheba	Queen of Sheba discovered the secrets of Solomon (1 Kings 10:17).
10	Esther	Esther's uncle advised her to keep her Jewish identity a secret (Esther 2:20).
11	Gehazi	Elisha's servant secretly returned to Naaman and accepted a gift from Naaman for his healing (2 Kings 5:21–23).
12	Daniel	God revealed secrets to Daniel concerning the interpretation of Nebuchadnezzar's dream (Daniel 2:19).

Table 2

The Secret Hall of Fame

		New Testament Secrets
1	Mary	Mary was impregnated by the Holy Ghost. Note the secrecy of this pregnancy (Luke 1:35).
2	Herod	Herod sought a secret meeting with the wise men to determine the exact birthplace of Jesus (Matthew 2:7).
3	Wise men	The wisemen were warned in a dream to keep the location of Jesus a secret (Matthew 2:7).
4	Jesus	Jesus hid in Egypt and didn't return until Herod died (Matthew 2:13–15).
5	Judas	Satan entered Judas" heart. Judas secretly betrayed Jesus (Luke 22:1).
6	Nicodemus	Nicodemous has a secret conference with Jesus. He wanted to know the secret of the kingdom (John 3:1–16).
7	Disciples	Disciples came to Jesus secretly. They wanted to know the secrets of the end time (Matthew 23:3).
8	Pilate's wife	Pilate's wife dreamed about Jesus. She knows the secret; she knows that Jesus is innocent (Matthew 27:19).
9	Ananias and Sapphira	A husband and wife stole money from the church. The secret was revealed by the Holy Spirit (Acts 5:1–12).
10	Saul/Paul	Paul received a glimpse of heaven. God instructed Paul not to tell the secret revelation (2 Corinthians 12:4).
11	The return of Jesus	The day and time that Jesus will return is a secret. No man knows the day or hour when Christ will return (Matthew 24:36).
12	Apostle John	From the Island of Patmos, Christ revealed the mysteries and secrets of his glory in Book of Revelations (Revelation 1:9-20).

Sons of Jacob

Mother	Birth order	Sons	Meaning of Names	Reference of Birth (Genesis)	Secret of the Sons	Symbol	Reference of Prophecy (Genesis)
L e a h	1	Reuben	"Behold, a Son"	29:32	Sexual Secrets	Water	49:3-4
	2	Simeon	"Hearing"	29:33	The Eavesdropper	Violence	49:5-7
	3	Levi	"Attachment"	29:34	Secret Relationship	Cruelty	49:5-7
	4	Judah	"Praise"	29:35	Secret Praise	Lion	49:8-12
B I L H A H	5	Dan	"Judgment"	30:6	Secret Justice of God	Serpent	49:16-18
	6	Naphtali	"Wrestle"	30:8	Secret Wrestling	Deer	49:21
Z I L P A H	7	Gad	"Good Fortune"	30:11	Secret Abundance	Raider	49:19
	8	Asher	"Happy"	30:13	Secret Happiness	Rich Food	49:20
L E A H	9	Issachar	"Reward"	30:18	Secret Rewards	Donkey	49:14-15
	10	Zebulun	"Abode"	30:20	Secret Places	Ships	49:13
R A C H E L	11	Joseph	"May he add"	30:24	Secret Dream	Fruitful	49:22-26
	12	Benjamin	"Son of my sorrow & Son of the right hand"	35:18	Secret insecurity	Wolf	49:27

REFERENCES TO OTHER SCRIPTURES
ON SECRETS

(my bold type)

- "My soul, come not thou into their *secret*; unto their assembly, mine honour, be not thou united: for in their anger they slew a man, and in their selfwill they digged down a wall." Genesis 49:6

- "Cursed be the man that maketh any graven or molten image, an abomination unto the LORD, the work of the hands of the craftsman, and putteth it in a *secret* place. And all the people shall answer and say, Amen." Deuteronomy 27:15

- "The *secret* things belong unto the LORD our God: but those things which are revealed belong unto us and to our children for ever, that we may do all the words of this law." Deuteronomy 29:29

- "But he himself turned again from the quarries that were by Gilgal, and said, I have a *secret* errand unto thee, O king: who said, Keep silence. And all that stood by him went out from him." Judges 3:19

- "And the angel of the LORD said unto him, Why askest thou thus after my name, seeing it is *secret*?" Judges 13:18

- "But Jonathan Saul's son delighted much in David: and Jonathan told David, saying, Saul my father seeketh to kill thee: now therefore, I pray thee, take heed to thyself until the morning, and abide in a *secret* place, and hide thyself." 1 Samuel 19:2

- "O that thou wouldest hide me in the grave, that thou wouldest keep me *secret*, until thy wrath be past, that thou wouldest appoint me a set time, and remember me!" Job 14:13

- "Hast thou heard the *secret* of God? and dost thou restrain wisdom to thyself?" Job 15:8

- "Are the consolations of God small with thee? is there any *secret* thing with thee?" Job 15:11

- "All darkness shall be hid in his *secret* places: a fire not blown shall consume him; it shall go ill with him that is left in his tabernacle." Job 20:26

- "As I was in the days of my youth, when the *secret* of God was upon my tabernacle;" Job 29:4

- "Hide them in the dust together; and bind their faces in *secret*." Job 40:13

- "He sitteth in the lurking places of the villages: in the *secret* places doth he murder the innocent: his eyes are privily set against the poor." Psalm 10:8

- "He lieth in wait *secretly* as a lion in his den: he lieth in wait to catch the poor: he doth catch the poor, when he draweth him into his net." Psalm 10:9

- "Like as a lion that is greedy of his prey, and as it were a young lion lurking in *secret* places." Psalm 17:12

- "He made darkness his *secret* place; his pavilion round about him were dark waters and thick clouds of the skies." Psalm 18:11

- "Who can understand his errors? cleanse thou me from *secret* faults." Psalm 19:12

- "The *secret* of the LORD is with them that fear him; and he will shew them his covenant." Psalm 25:14

- "For in the time of trouble he shall hide me in his pavilion: in the *secret* of his tabernacle shall he hide me; he shall set me up upon a rock." Psalm 27:5

- "Thou shalt hide them in the *secret* of thy presence from the pride of man: thou shalt keep them *secretly* in a pavilion from the strife of tongues." Psalm 31:20

- "Shall not God search this out? for he knoweth the *secrets* of the heart." Psalm 44:21

- "Hide me from the *secret* counsel of the wicked; from the insurrection of the workers of iniquity:" Psalm 64:2

- "That they may shoot in *secret* at the perfect: suddenly do they shoot at him, and fear not." Psalm 64:4

- "Thou calledst in trouble, and I delivered thee; I answered thee in the *secret* place of thunder: I proved thee at the waters of Meribah. Selah." Psalm 81:7

- "Thou hast set our iniquities before thee, our *secret* sins in the light of thy countenance." Psalm 90:8

- "He that dwelleth in the *secret* place of the most High shall abide under the shadow of the Almighty." Psalm 91:1

- "My substance was not hid from thee, when I was made in *secret*, and curiously wrought in the lowest parts of the earth." Psalm 139:15

- "For the froward is abomination to the LORD: but his *secret* is with the righteous." Proverbs 3:32

- "Stolen waters are sweet, and bread eaten in *secret* is pleasant." Proverbs 9:17

- "A talebearer revealeth *secrets*: but he that is of a faithful spirit concealeth the matter." Proverbs 11:13

- "He that goeth about as a talebearer revealeth *secrets*: therefore meddle not with him that flattereth with his lips." Proverbs 20:19

- "A gift in *secret* pacifieth anger: and a reward in the bosom strong wrath." Proverbs 21:14

- "Debate thy cause with thy neighbour himself; and discover not a *secret* to another." Proverbs 25:9

- "Open rebuke is better than *secret* love." Proverbs 27:5

- "For God shall bring every work into judgment, with every *secret* thing, whether it be good, or whether it be evil." Ecclesiastes 12:14

- "O my dove, that art in the clefts of the rock, in the *secret* places of the stairs, let me see thy countenance, let me hear thy voice; for sweet is thy voice, and thy countenance is comely." Song of Solomon 2:14

- "And I will give thee the treasures of darkness, and hidden riches of *secret* places, that thou mayest know that I, the

LORD, which call thee by thy name, am the God of Israel." Isaiah 45:3

- "I have not spoken in *secret*, in a dark place of the earth: I said not unto the seed of Jacob, Seek ye me in vain: I the LORD speak righteousness, I declare things that are right. Isaiah 45:19

- "Come ye near unto me, hear ye this; I have not spoken in *secret* from the beginning; from the time that it was, there am I: and now the Lord GOD, and his Spirit, hath sent me." Isaiah 48:16

- "Also in thy skirts is found the blood of the souls of the poor innocents: I have not found it by *secret* search, but upon all these." Jeremiah 2:34

- "But if ye will not hear it, my soul shall weep in *secret* places for your pride; and mine eye shall weep sore, and run down with tears, because the LORD's flock is carried away captive." Jeremiah 13:17

- "Can any hide himself in *secret* places that I shall not see him? saith the LORD. Do not I fill heaven and earth? saith the LORD." Jeremiah 23:24

- "But I have made Esau bare, I have uncovered his *secret* places, and he shall not be able to hide himself: his seed is spoiled, and his brethren, and his neighbours, and he is not." Jeremiah 49:10

- "He was unto me as a bear lying in wait, and as a lion in *secret* places." Lamentations 3:10

- "My face will I turn also from them, and they shall pollute my *secret* place: for the robbers shall enter into it, and defile it." Ezekiel 7:22

- "Behold, thou art wiser than Daniel; there is no *secret* that they can hide from thee:" Ezekiel 28:3

- "That they would desire mercies of the God of heaven concerning this *secret*; that Daniel and his fellows should not perish with the rest of the wise men of Babylon." Daniel 2:18

- "Then was the *secret* revealed unto Daniel in a night vision. Then Daniel blessed the God of heaven." Daniel 2:19

- "He revealeth the deep and *secret* things: he knoweth what is in the darkness, and the light dwelleth with him." Daniel 2:22

- "Daniel answered in the presence of the king, and said, The *secret* which the king hath demanded cannot the wise men, the astrologers, the magicians, the soothsayers, shew unto the king; But there is a God in heaven that revealeth *secrets*, and maketh known to the king Nebuchadnezzar what shall be in the latter days. Thy dream, and the visions of thy head upon thy bed, are these; As for thee, O king, thy thoughts came into thy mind upon thy bed, what should come to pass hereafter: and he that revealeth *secrets* maketh known to thee what shall come to pass. But as for me, this *secret* is not revealed to me for any wisdom that I have more than any living, but for their sakes that shall make known the interpretation to the king, and that thou mightest know the thoughts of thy heart." Daniel 2:27-30

- "The king answered unto Daniel, and said, Of a truth it is, that your God is a God of gods, and a Lord of kings, and a revealer of **secrets,** seeing thou couldest reveal this *secret*." Daniel 2:47

- "Belteshazzar, master of the magicians, because I know that the spirit of the holy gods is in thee, and no *secret* troubleth thee, tell me the visions of my dream that I have seen, and the interpretation thereof." Daniel 4:9

- "Surely the Lord GOD will do nothing, but he revealeth his *secret* unto his servants the prophets." Amos 3:7

- "That thine alms may be in *secret*: and thy Father which seeth in *secret* himself shall reward thee openly." Matthew 6:4

- "But thou, when thou prayest, enter into thy closet, and when thou hast shut thy door, pray to thy Father which is in *secret*; and thy Father which seeth in *secret* shall reward thee openly." Matthew 6:6

- "That thou appear not unto men to fast, but unto thy Father which is in *secret*: and thy Father, which seeth in *secret*, shall reward thee openly." Matthew 6:18

- "That it might be fulfilled which was spoken by the prophet, saying, I will open my mouth in parables; I will utter things which have been kept *secret* from the foundation of the world." Matthew 13:35

- "Wherefore if they shall say unto you, Behold, he is in the desert; go not forth: behold, he is in the *secret* chambers; believe it not." Matthew 24:26

- "For nothing is *secret*, that shall not be made manifest; neither any thing hid, that *shall* not be known and come abroad." Luke 8:17

- "No man, when he hath lighted a candle, putteth it in a *secret* place, neither under a bushel, but on a candlestick, that they which come in may see the light." Luke 11:33

- "For there is no man that doeth any thing in *secret*, and he himself seeketh to be known openly. If thou do these things, shew thyself to the world." John 7:4

- "But when his brethren were gone up, then went he also up unto the feast, not openly, but as it were in *secret*." John 7:10

- "And after this Joseph of Arimathaea, being a disciple of Jesus, but *secretly* for fear of the Jews, besought Pilate that he might take away the body of Jesus: and Pilate gave him leave. He came therefore, and took the body of Jesus." John 19:38

- "In the day when God shall judge the *secrets* of men by Jesus Christ according to my gospel." Romans 2:16

- "Jesus answered him, I spake openly to the world; I ever taught in the synagogue, and in the temple, whither the Jews always resort; and in *secret* have I said nothing." John 18:20

- "Now to him that is of power to stablish you according to my gospel, and the preaching of Jesus Christ, according to the revelation of the mystery, which was kept *secret* since the world began." Romans 16:25

- "And thus are the **secrets** of his heart made manifest; and so falling down on his face he will worship God, and report that God is in you of a truth." 1 Corinthians 14:25

- "For it is a shame even to speak of those things which are done of them in **secret**." Ephesians 5:12

BIBLIOGRAPHY

Abbott, Louis. *Analytical Study of Words*, unknown binding, 1996.

Aftergood, Steven. *"On Leaks of National Security Secrets: A Response to Michael Hurt."* National Security Studies Quarterly 8 (Winter 2002): 97-102.

Alsop, John R. *Index to the Revised Bauer-Arndt-Gingrich Greek Lexicon, An.* Grand Rapids, MI: Zondervan, 1981.

Andrew, Christopher. *For the President's Eyes Only: Secret Intelligence and the American Presidency from Washington to Bush.* New York: HarperCollins, 1995. 660 pp. (JK468 I6A844 1995).

Begley, Sharon. "Do You Hear What I Hear?" *Newsweek*, Special Summer Edition, 1991, 14.

Behn, Aphra. The *Works of Aphra Behn, III: The Fair Jilt and Other Stories.* Janet Todd, ed. Columbus, OH: Ohio State UP, 1995. (Aphra Behn, 1640-1689, was the first professional woman writer in English literature).

Bible Translations:
    Amplified Version
    King James Version
    New International Version
    New King James Version
    New Living Translation

Eban, Abba Solomon. *Eban, Abba: An Autobiography.* London: Weidenfeld and Nicolson, 1977.

Franklin, Benjamin (alias Richard Saunders). *Poor Richard's Almanack*, coded, edited and translated by Rich Hall for the Independence Hall Web site, book Publishers in White Plains, NY Peter Pauper Press, Incorporated November, 1983.

Georg, Friedrich. *Hitler's Miracle Weapons: Secret Nuclear Weapons of the Third Reich and Their Carrier Systems*. Vol. 1. England. Helion and Company. December, 2004.

Ginzberg, Louis. *Legends of the Bible*. Philadelphia-Jerusalem: The Jewish Publication Society, 2001.

Havner, Vance. Quoted by Pastor Steve Jackson New Song Community Church, Cumming, GA Sermon: Topic: *Busyness*. August 18, 2002.

Hybels, Bill. *Courageous Leadership*. Grand Rapids, MI: Zondervan, August, 2002.

Jenkins, Phillip. *Beyond Tolerance, Child Pornography on the Internet*. New York, NY: NYU Press, 2001.

Kann, Robert. "Alliances versus Ententes," *World Politics*, 28(1976): 614.

Kennedy, John F. *Address to the Central Intelligence Agency*. 28 November 1961.

King, Martin Luther. "I have a dream" speech delivered in Washington DC *at Civil Rights March on Washington*. August 28, 1963.

Merriam-Webster's Dictionary. July, 2004. Print.

Mulrine, Anna, and Nancy Bentrup. "The Power of Secrets." *U.S. News & World Report*. 134 (27 January 2003): 48-50.

Unger, Merrill R. K. *New Unger's Bible Dictionary*. May, 2006.

Russett, Bruce M. "Pearl Harbor: Deterrence Theory and Decision Theory," *Journal of Peace Research*, 4 (1967): 104.

Schooler, Jayne. *Searching for a Past: The Adopted Adult's Unique Process of Finding Identity.* Bedford, OH: Pinion Press, 1995.

Stevenson, Robert Louis. *Dr. Jekyll and Mr. Hyde.* London: Longmans, Green and Co., 1886.

Waldenmaier, Jacob Louis. *What Has Happened to Awe?* Article written by Jacob Louis, 2004. http://members.aol.com/jacoblouis/awe.htm.

Youngblood, Ronald F. *Nelson's Illustrated Bible Dictionary.* May, 2006.

Waggner, George. *The Wolf Man,* Universal Pictures. 12 December 1941.

World Book Encyclopedia, The. 1994. Print.

CPSIA information can be obtained
at www.ICGtesting.com
Printed in the USA
FFHW021948260719
53898407-59616FF